The CGNET Story

THE CGNET STORY

A CASE STUDY OF
INTERNATIONAL COMPUTER NETWORKING

Georg Lindsey
Ken Novak
Selçuk Ozgediz
and
David Balson

INTERNATIONAL DEVELOPMENT RESEARCH CENTRE
Ottawa • Cairo • Dakar • Johannesburg • Montevideo • Nairobi
New Delhi • Singapore

Published by the International Development Research Centre
PO Box 8500, Ottawa, ON, Canada K1G 3H9

© International Development Research Centre 1994

Lindsey, G.
Novak, K.
Ozgediz, S.
Balson, D.

CGNET story : a case study in international computer networking.
Ottawa, ON, IDRC, 1993. xii + 127 p. : ill.

/Computer conferencing/, /communication engineering/, /information
networks/, /information technology/, /agricultural research/, /research
centres/ — /data collecting/, /data transmission/, /telecommunications/,
/future/, references.

UDC: 621.391:681.31   ISBN: 0-88936-678-0

A microfiche edition is available.

CONTENTS

FOREWORD

This book provides a great deal of organizational and technical information and should interest a wide audience. I thought, however, that some readers might benefit from a bit of personal insight into CGNET, the electronic mail network of the Consultative Group on International Agricultural Research (CGIAR). I have been involved in CGNET, in an entirely nontechnical way, from the start and have become a devoted, almost daily user. These few words, therefore, leave issues of broader significance to the book itself and address more modest matters.

The first suggestion I heard to link the CGIAR centres electronically was made in the mid-1970s by the distinguished communication scientist Ithiel de Sola Poole of the Massachusetts Institute of Technology (MIT). He suggested to the education specialists at the United States Agency for International Development (USAID) that the relatively new technology of packet switching — the rapid transmission over telephone lines of data in condensed form — could be employed in a polling system that used a network of computers linked through the international telephone system. One central computer would place two rounds of telephone calls daily to each of a set of smaller computers. On the first round, mail from each of the centres would be collected for central sorting. On the second round, the sorted mail would be sent to the addressees.

As the person supervising both the United States participation in CGIAR and the central USAID education function, I had to be persuaded that this concept should be explored. I recall being somewhat resistant, on the grounds that CGIAR was already taking a lot of risks with new technology directly relevant to its mandate. I also thought that the centres did not have a requirement for a lot of communication with each other, or with the central organs of CGIAR, and should not divert effort into the risky field of international communications. Before long, however, I found the excitement of the idea catching and agreed that it should be pursued. About a year later, I was disappointed to learn that it had foundered on the unwillingness of too many national telephone authorities to authorize the use of their circuits for this purpose.

I had no occasion to think about the matter further until I took over as Executive Secretary of CGIAR toward the end of 1982. I learned from my deputy, Peter Greening, that, because the communications problem was on its way to being solved and the technology was coming into commercial use, the International Development Research Centre (IDRC) was willing to support an experiment with the use of electronic mail (e-mail). IDRC was seeking to work with an international institution with far-flung branches, and CGIAR was its first choice. Peter was surprised how easy I was to persuade. As my enthusiasm came to the surface, he wisely counselled that we needed to proceed cautiously in selling the idea to the international agricultural research centres, lest they think it an effort to assert unwanted bureaucratic control in violation of the first principle of the CGIAR system: defence of centre autonomy.

Some of the centres were indeed suspicious, and others showed a distinct lack of enthusiasm, but enough of the directors sensed the opportunity that was being presented. Once the decision was made to proceed, the centres turned to the Secretariat to manage the experiment. From then on, the problem was one of moving fast enough. The experiment quickly turned into application. Moreover, many organizations moved to make use of e-mail at the national and international level. CGIAR leadership became somewhat less distinct than we had hoped.

Although CGNET quickly became routine in parts of the CGIAR system, there were many challenges to deal with, and in fact some have not yet yielded. The Government of Syria will not permit ICARDA (the International Center for Agricultural Research in the Dry Areas) to participate in CGNET for security reasons. Local telephone communications, covering the few kilometres from the centre to the satellite ground station, still constitute a bottleneck that frustrates users in a number of places. The difficulty of getting through to an overloaded local telephone number during business hours prevents one centre from making extensive use of the system.

The story of the growth of CGNET is very much one of the exercise of personal ingenuity to overcome problems. In some places, the drive to take advantage of the opportunity was strong in a centre director, a computer chief, or an individual scientist, and the problems melted. In others, there was no enthusiastic entrepreneur, and problems seemed insurmountable. In this story, as in everything else, the centres in the CGIAR system are all individual: no one centre is really like any other.

One of the biggest differences among the users of CGNET relates to the interface of the individual with the system. The strongest personal impact comes when users operate their own microcomputers to engage CGNET directly. (This is the category into which I have been lucky enough to fall.) When you open your own mailbox two or three times a day and look at messages that lack any dimension of distance — one from Manila is identical in form to one from across the city or the office — there is an immediacy of communication that can have a major impact on work habits. Incoming messages can be, and often are, acted on as soon as they are read. One can look up relevant facts, or think over an issue, and still respond within a few minutes. Communication through the CGNET takes place in an interactive or conversational mode that changes the perception of relationships with correspondents to one of nearness, even if they are physically far away.

Those collaborating at a distance on manuscripts can achieve this feeling of nearness even without using CGNET directly, provided they have access to the common work in the form of a word processor file that can be revised and then exchanged any number of times. Use of a personal computer combined with CGNET is the key to this kind of benefit.

The most precocious CGNET users are those whose mailboxes literally travel with them. To achieve this, the users need to go to places where access to the system is open to individuals (such as centres or institutions using the Dialcom system). They can then read and send mail as if they were at home. In the absence of such an institutional base, they must overcome barriers in each country by knowing both the correct telephone number and code, and by having the equipment to tap into the telephone system. For these people, the CGNET communication really is personal, and the mailbox is open for them wherever they happen to be.

A far greater number in CGIAR interact with CGNET indirectly, receiving printed text at their desks and providing answers on paper, or possibly as a computer file, to be copied into the system. For them, there is little difference between CGNET and the telex or the facsimile, except that there are no real limitations on the size of documents. The CGNET will not transmit pictures, but it does produce a more legible output than facsimile. Some people may prefer a facsimile because they perceive it to be more personal than either CGNET or telex because it sends an exact copy of what they have written. If one starts with information already on a piece of paper, facsimile is faster and does not require the recipient to "log on."

To work with CGNET effectively, it is important to know something about your correspondents. Are they looking at a screen and tapping out a reply? Are they looking at a piece of paper that may get to them many hours after being read in the computer (most of the time being spent in interoffice mail)? There is no source for this kind of information in the CGNET directories. One learns the sort of relationship others have to the system only through use and observation.

A further pleasure of my own involvement with CGNET was being associated with linking the system to the World Bank internal e-mail structure. Once again, we were in luck. We needed an inter-link technology just as it was about to come onto the market. My immediate motivation was personal: I did not like to open two mailboxes every morning, one looking out at the world of the CGIAR and the other at the Bank. The link was achieved and has been very beneficial. However, it involved some cost of immediacy so far as CGNET was concerned because messages are sent between the two systems only four times a day — something I have found easy to forget, to my embarrassment. There is no appraisal yet of the value of the entire agricultural community at the World Bank being able to communicate efficiently with the CGIAR system, but it must surely be large. Beyond that, the Bank gained the ability to establish exchanges with the much broader world of users of Dialcom services. All that is necessary to reach into a world much broader than agriculture is a mutual exchange of addresses.

Joining to provide the story of CGNET are four persons who have been intimately involved, all in different roles. David Balson of IDRC provided the link to early work on the use of computer-based message systems and was the one who brought the long-standing IDRC initiative to test the methodology through the CGIAR to fruition. Georg Lindsey was the consultant chosen to undertake the feasibility study. He worked through the initial problems and has never stopped driving the system forward to new accomplishments. Along the way, he formed CGNET Services International, a private company that is the mainstay of current operations. Ken Novak was an early recruit for implementing the ideal. Georg called on him to travel wherever necessary around the world to help the centres deal with the wide variety of problems they faced in actually making it happen. He is still performing that role. Selcuk Ozgediz, Management Advisor in the CGIAR Secretariat, provided the active link between the CGIAR system and those who were building the CGNET structure. Among the four of them, they have knowledge in depth and different perspectives that are combined in this book to produce a comprehensive account of a real adventure in applying communications technology.

New adventures certainly lie ahead for the CGNET system and for the users of international electronic communication in general. It is with pride and pleasure that I commend to you the story of CGNET as an example of what can be done and of the many ways, expected and unexpected, in which people respond to new possibilities of communication.

Curtis Farrar
Executive Secretary (former)
CGIAR Secretariat
Washington, DC

ACKNOWLEDGMENTS

The authors wish to thank the many people at IDRC, the CGIAR Secretariat, and CGNET Services International Inc. who helped to bring this book to fruition. In particular, we wish to thank Kristin Kerrigan of CGNET Services International Inc. for her varied and valuable contributions to the manuscript.

Chapter 1

THE ORIGINS OF CGNET

World food production in the last decade has barely kept up with ever-increasing demand. This is especially true in the developing countries, where population growth has led to increased imports of basic foods. This in turn has resulted in higher prices, deeper poverty, and, in some countries, the threat of starvation. Arable land is quickly disappearing because of spreading urbanization, soil degradation, salinity, and scarcity of water, factors that may limit the ability of exporting countries to keep up with the demand for food.

Meeting the growing demand for food by developing nations is a problem that will confront the international community beyond the year 2000. In fact, the situation could easily be more severe by then. All reasonable alternatives must be considered in a search for solutions. The authors of this book believe that one promising alternative is to increase the effectiveness of the scientific research community. Advances in agricultural technology will certainly be a key to survival, but research and supporting technologies will be important as well. Effective research requires rapid and reliable information exchange. In particular, communications technology must be exploited as a tool to assist scientists, researchers, planners, and administrators. Timely and accurate scientific decisions may have far-reaching effects worth millions of dollars and, more importantly, may save many lives.

This book describes the design and development of an international computer-based messaging system for a scientific research network, the Consultative Group on International Agricultural Research (CGIAR), whose centres and remote facilities are located primarily in developing countries. The goal of this activity was, and is, to improve scientific, administrative, and information services-oriented communication within CGIAR, with the ultimate aim of improving the effectiveness of the international agricultural research system. The result of the project was CGNET, a network that has been in daily use since 1984.

The Consultative Group on International Agricultural Research

CGIAR is an international consortium sponsored jointly by the World Bank, the United Nations Development Programme (UNDP), and the Food and Agriculture Organization of the United Nations (FAO). Its mandate is to support research programs aimed at improving the quantity and quality of food produced in developing nations. These programs are carried out by 18 autonomous international agricultural research centres (IARCs) located in Colombia, Côte d'Ivoire, Ethiopia, France, India, Indonesia, Italy, Kenya, Mexico, the Netherlands, Nigeria, Peru, the Philippines, Sri Lanka, Syria, and the United States. Each centre, in turn, has experimental stations and regional offices that bring the total to at least 100 remote sites in over 60 countries.

The CGIAR centres and two secretariats (the CGIAR Secretariat located at the World Bank in Washington and the Technical Advisory Committee (TAC) Secretariat located at FAO in Rome) employ about 1 100 scientists and engineers, 100 administrators, and 70 library staff. The total staff, including all classifications (such as professional, support, clerical, farm staff, guards, and technicians) and personnel at remote sites, amounts to approximately 15 000 people.

The International Development Research Centre

IDRC, Canada's International Development Research Centre, was created by the Canadian Parliament in 1970. Its mandate is to provide funds and expert advice for development-related research that is in accordance with the individual needs and priorities of Third

World countries. IDRC is funded by the people of Canada and is an autonomous organization that reports to Canada's Parliament. It operates under the direction of an international Board of Governors.

The operations of IDRC are based on the premise that the greatest understanding of a country's problems comes from within that country and that solutions must be appropriate to its people, resources, culture, priorities, and aspirations. For the most part, IDRC supports projects that are identified, designed, conducted, and managed by researchers in developing countries.

IDRC's mission is to contribute to economic and social development through research and activities that support research. It emphasizes applied research directly relevant to basic human needs. All activities are aimed at supporting a development process based on sustainable growth, equity, and participation.

To fulfill its mandate most effectively, IDRC is organized to support five distinct fields: Environment and Natural Resources; Social Sciences; Health Sciences; Information Sciences and Systems; and Corporate Affairs and Initiatives. At the United Nations Conference on Environment and Development (UNCED) in June 1992, IDRC was chosen as a key implementing agency for Agenda 21.

Computer-Based Communications Technology

A promising communications technique, which has been used extensively since the beginning of the 1970s, is the computer-based messaging system (CBMS). In these systems, users compose messages at a computer terminal and then transmit the message, along with addressing information, to a central "host" computer using telecommunications links. The host computer stores the message until the recipient calls that computer, logs on, and receives any messages that are waiting. In addition to providing almost instantaneous communication, a CBMS is generally much less expensive than traditional forms of communication (such as telex). A CBMS is flexible. It allows the use of individualized message formatting styles (as well as the use of both upper and lower case characters) and offers practical options such as message forwarding, automatic acknowledgment of message receipt, and delivery of a single message to multiple addresses.

As an extension of this feature, designers developed computer-based conferencing systems that allow "many-to-many" communications on specific topics. Computer conferencing systems enable groups of people scattered throughout the world to discuss topics of common interest. They also provide a quick way to distribute and obtain feedback on agendas or documents before or after scheduled meetings. The storage, retrieval, and processing capabilities of the computer, coupled with the appropriate software, permit the management and tracking of messages in the computer conference. A computer with conferencing software can manage many conferences simultaneously as well as allow person-to-person messaging. In effect, one can participate in a "plenary" session of a conference discussion (computer conferencing) and engage in "corridor chatter" (computer-based messaging) at the same time. Conferences can be set up as public conferences (open to all those with access) or as private conferences (open only to those who have been registered as participants). Some computer conferencing systems have additional features that allow joint authorship of papers, cross-referencing and selective retrieval of text, and even a voting facility for consensus gathering.

Perhaps the key characteristic of computer conferences is their asynchronous nature (senders and recipients communicate using the computer at times of their choosing). Certain advantages ensue. Problems of communicating across time zones and the frustrations of trying to make connections over the telephone are minimized. One is able to participate in a number of electronic conferences while conducting regular work. Individuals are able to ensure greater accuracy in their communications because they communicate while remaining close to their own data sources. In effect, the quality of communication is improved as individuals control the location, time, and rate of their communications. Computer conferencing has also nurtured information transfers and new contacts that would not have taken place with traditional means alone.

Systems offering messaging and conferencing services have

been available through academic institutions, private companies, and telecommunications authorities since the early 1970s. In some cases, these have been internal "free" services; in other cases, they have been offered on a commercial basis. The number of services and the variety of modalities of use have grown dramatically over the past 20 years.

Two of the best known and widely used teleconferencing systems are Cosy at Guelph University in Canada and EIES (Electronic Information Exchange System) at the New Jersey Institute of Technology in the United States. The predominant academic electronic-mail (e-mail) systems in the United States are the Internet and BITNET systems.

In the CGNET project, commercially available e-mail systems were used because international access to these systems tended to be more widely available and because speed and reliability were higher. In 1985, there were few choices. Now there are many commercial offerings, including ATT Mail, MCI Mail, Dialcom (BT Tymnet), Sprintmail, CompuServe, and others.

The commercial or academic systems are not defined. Rather, a Bibliography is presented that describes the various conferencing and e-mail systems. One of the most comprehensive presentations is Quarterman (1990).

Packet Switching

Communication between individuals is characterized by bursts. In fact, it has been estimated that over 60% of a typical conversation involves silent periods. In circuit-switched systems, such as those that handle conventional telex messages or telephone conversations, a fixed bandwidth is allotted and kept open for the duration of the call. This means that a physical connection is maintained between the two points, with an obvious waste of transmission resources.

Packet switching, on the other hand, is based on sharing of a communication channel among many users in proportion to the amount of data they have to send. Packet switching was developed initially for interactive applications with computers (for example, on-line database retrieval). Communications sent by a terminal are broken into short packets, and source, destination, and serial information are attached to each packet. Packets are transmitted by the most appropriate available route by "nodes" (specialized computers) in the network. The packets are retransmitted if an acknowledgment of reception from any node is not received. The packets are reassembled at the destination. The network is shared by many users and bandwidth is not exclusively reserved for any one user.

Packet switching is a more reliable, secure, and speedier method of transmitting information, and its cost is based more on the quantity of information transferred than on time or distance. The continuing expansion of both national and international packet-switching networks has played a major role in the increasing use of computer-based communication techniques. In places where local packet-switching networks are not available, international networks can be reached by using modems and the conventional telephone system. In particularly difficult or remote locations, data can be sent using satellite or radio technology.

IDRC Workshop on Computer-Based Conferencing

In 1981, one member of IDRC's Board of Governors, Carl-Goran Heden, and the Director of the former Information Sciences Division, John Woolston, began discussing the merits and importance of computer-based communication techniques for development. They concluded that these new communication techniques were being used more and more in the industrialized world and they expressed the concern that Third World institutions might be left out of the design, implementation, and use of these rapidly expanding computer networks. To explore state-of-the-art technology and receive advice on any potential role for donors, IDRC convened a week-long workshop in October 1981 (Balson et al. 1981). It was perhaps indicative of the need for that workshop that only isolated pockets of activity in this field could be found in developing countries.

Experts from Brazil, India, international organizations involved in the informatics field, and those involved with existing systems discussed the structure of current and proposed systems, their advantages and disadvantages, impediments to implementation, and possibilities for their use in developing countries.

The consensus of the workshop was that these systems would be an integral part of the available communications options in the coming decade and that unless the developing nations could participate in this electronic community of science and technology, they would suffer from a serious disenfranchisement. This might take the form of limited or no access to the information resources of the developed nations, or the inability to gain timely access to results and techniques found in the developing countries themselves.

The participants at the meeting felt that there was a role for donors to play in this area and identified the need for a sufficient base of knowledge and experience related to these new information technologies. Accordingly, within the Information Sciences Division of IDRC, a modest program in the area of telecommunications systems was established. More specifically, the focus of this program was on data communication techniques in support of research activities. Its objective was (and is) to facilitate and support developing-country involvement in the testing, experimentation, development, and use of these techniques and thus to enable developing country institutions to make informed decisions on the suitability of these techniques for their needs.

In the earliest phase of the program, priority was placed on two exercises. The first was the initiation, organization, coordination, and evaluation of an International Computer-Based Conference on the Bioconversion of Lignocellulosics. The second was a demonstration project, with a prominent international research group, that led to the activities described in this book.

Computer-Based Communication for CGIAR

To establish its telecommunications program, IDRC considered it was necessary to demonstrate the advantages of data communication with an established group that could influence national governments and their telecommunications authorities. Such a demonstration might stimulate a multiplier effect within other international groups. CGIAR seemed the most logical group for a demonstration project because it had been making important progress globally in the field of agricultural development. Moreover, IDRC had a direct interest, having invested over 30 million Canadian dollars (CAD) (approximately 23 million United States dollars (USD)) in 83 projects with CGIAR during the previous 13 years. IDRC felt that a successful demonstration project would encourage research in the developing countries in the field of telematics.

There was an additional strong reason for identifying this network. For a number of years, the CGIAR system, or others on their behalf, had been considering data communication to facilitate scientific and administrative communication among the centres. In 1976, MIT conducted a study entitled "Low Cost Data and Text Communication for the Less Developed Countries," with a special emphasis on the IARCs. In 1978, USAID funded a follow-up study, performed by CRC Systems, Inc., entitled "A Low Cost Data Communications System for the CGIAR: A Report on Feasibility with a Preliminary Design." Although both reports concluded that such systems were feasible and recommended follow-up action, no implementation ensued. The delay was due to timing problems and, to some extent, to the potential of legal or regulatory constraints and to unproven implementation strategies.

In the early 1980s, within CGIAR, conventional communication costs were rising, budgets were shrinking, the need for international scientific and administrative communication was increasing, and a greater number of technical solutions were available. Following discussions with IDRC, CGIAR decided that it was time to reassess the technical, legal, administrative, and economic feasibility of implementing a data-transfer network for the IARCs. To that end, an IDRC staff member was invited to discuss this topic at the IARC Directors' meeting in Washington in November 1982. At this meeting, the Directors encouraged IDRC to take the lead and manage a feasibility study on implementing a data-transfer network for the CGIAR system. The Directors, for their part, appointed a steering committee to guide the study. Although it was pointed out that the major communication needs for any particular centre were between that centre and its remote field sites, it was agreed to look first at a system to handle intercentre communication needs. The experience and knowledge gained from establishing a less complex system could then be used to tackle the more difficult, but higher return situation of intracentre communication.

Following these meetings, IDRC sought appropriate consultants. After a lengthy search, Telematics International, a California-based consulting organization with partners in the United Kingdom and Australia, was chosen. The individuals were exceptionally well-qualified to carry out the work. The principal American consultant had established the first commercial computer-conferencing service in the United States. The British partner was very experienced in dealing with governmental regulatory agencies, having helped in the design of computer-based message systems for British Telecom and for the Government of Ontario. Another American partner was an expert in needs assessment, design, implementation, and evaluation of integrated office systems.

The feasibility study funded and managed by IDRC was broken into two phases to allow the results of the first phase to be presented at the IARC Directors' meeting in Tunisia in July 1983. Because the study was split into two parts, the participants in the meeting would receive a fully documented account of the first phase and would have an opportunity, if necessary, to reorient the consultants before they started the second phase.

To guide the study, IDRC provided a document entitled "Guidelines for a Feasibility Study on the Implementation of a Data Transfer Network for the International Agricultural Research Centers." The document specified that four basic areas needed to be examined:

➤ **Communication needs** — including both current and future needs, communication volume and cost patterns, various communication media (including travel, telephone, and telex), and external database searching;

➤ **Technical possibilities** — including microcomputers, e-mail, computer conferencing, and telecommunication options, with consideration of developing or purchasing software, and hiring services;

➤ **Implementation feasibility** — including the technical, legal, regulatory, administrative, and economic aspects for each centre (hardware and interconnection requirements, national communication policies, training and monitoring requirements, and a cost–benefit analysis); and

➤ **Conclusion and recommendations** — including a system design and a plan of action, covering timing, geographic extent, speed, capacity, costs, and mix of technologies.

A four-fold approach was developed. First, a "communication audit" of CGIAR staff was conducted to determine their communication needs. Second, the existing CGIAR communication traffic volume and flows were examined. Third, the existing array of technical alternatives for instituting a computer-based communications system was considered. Fourth, the technical resources of CGIAR were assessed to determine which in-place equipment could be used to facilitate the establishment and growth of the network. These four sets of information were synthesized to identify and recommend the communications technology and implementation procedures most appropriate for CGIAR.

The communication audit provided valuable information on the communication needs of CGIAR. Each year, 2 million USD was spent to make 21 600 international telephone calls, send 61 560 telexes and 30 720 telegrams, and mail almost a million letters and documents. Both scientists and administrators were interested in gaining access to remote international electronic messaging, the ability to send facsimiles of documents or letters to international locations, and the ability to reduce international telephone costs. Scientists also wanted statistical analysis capabilities and the ability to access remote databases. The strongest need was expressed for hard facts and specific data rather than for interpersonal communication. Fifty-six percent of the responding centres indicated a preference for a trained intermediary performing bibliographic database searches, whereas 44% preferred direct access (see Appendix 1 for survey results).

The initial analysis of the responses from the IARCs to the communication audit suggested that the target group of 13 centres and two secretariats should be extended to include some of the more important remote sites where more than one centre conducted research. Communications with these remote sites were particularly difficult and caused delays in developing research programs and in transmitting the resulting data. However, if the network had not been expanded to include these remote sites, it would have been difficult to realize its full potential, and the capacity of the new network might have been insufficient to handle the traffic demands created when these remote sites were later added. Furthermore, without the information obtained from this proposed study, it would have been very difficult to effectively plan for future network development.

During the first phase of the feasibility study, Telematics International concluded that the primary services of a CGIAR data-transfer network should be CBMS and gateway facilities from the CBMS to on-line database services. It was also determined that the prospects of fully implementing a CGIAR data-transfer network would be enhanced if a CBMS pilot project were established. A pilot project would maintain and strengthen the momentum that existed within the CGIAR system to implement new communication technologies. Because international CBMS existed at the time, some, but not all, of the centres could participate with little or no need to acquire new equipment or technology. Implementing a pilot project would expose the centres and the secretariats to some of the practical problems and implications of establishing a system-wide network. They would also have the opportunity to review the managerial and financial implications of using CBMS and a stronger basis for judging any recommendation regarding full network implementation.

The results of the first phase were presented for scrutiny and discussion at the IARC Directors' meeting in Tunisia. The Directors heartily endorsed the results and requested that the feasibility study be completed to build a firm foundation for a complete CGIAR network. Following the advice of the IARC directors, the CGIAR Secretariat committed funds for the proposed pilot project and Telematics International was chosen for the contract. The Secretariat stipulated that the study be expanded to include locations other than the centres themselves and locations where field experiments were carried out.

Accordingly, a project was designed with the CGIAR Secretariat as the executing agency and IDRC and CGIAR as the funding agencies. The first objective was to establish and evaluate a small CBMS pilot network for the CGIAR system. The project was to include training of relevant personnel at seven CGIAR locations: the International Board for Plant Genetic Resources (IBPGR) in Rome, the International Centre for Maize and Wheat Improvement (CIMMYT) in Mexico, the International Food Policy Research Institute (IFPRI) in Washington, DC, the International Rice Research Institute (IRRI) in Los Baños, Philippines, the International Service for National Agricultural Research (ISNAR) in The Hague, and the CGIAR and TAC secretariats. It was also to employ an internationally available CBMS. The second objective was to study the feasibility of a wider network. This wider network might include sites of special interest (such as research centres that were not formal members of CGIAR and other centres that had particular communications problems).

The CBMS Pilot Project and Evaluation

After a review of the many CBMS services that were commercially available at the time, the Dialcom system (now owned by BT Tymnet) was chosen. This choice was based on both financial and logistic considerations. From the outset, an outside service seemed most appropriate for the CGIAR system. Adopting an existing commercial service would minimize delays in implementing the pilot project and would allow results from actual use to be evaluated quickly. If the pilot project showed that a small or medium-sized network was most appropriate, the use of an outside service would also probably be the most cost-effective option. The high cost of setting up the physical infrastructure for a telecommunications network would not be justified if services were provided just to a small user group. In addition, using an outside service would allow the CGIAR network to take advantage of innovations developed for commercial users without having to create or install them itself. Finally, there was little desire to purchase equipment or to organize staff in a central location to administer the network, especially during the pilot study. The independent nature of the CGIAR institutes also indicated that, in the long run, outside services would be a better option than services owned and operated by the CGIAR Secretariat.

The Dialcom system was judged most suitable for CGIAR because of its orientation toward special-interest user groups and its favourable pricing. At that time, Dialcom also supported a United States Department of Agriculture user group that included several major agricultural universities. Because any Dialcom user could exchange messages with any other user, even with those in a different user group, the CGIAR network began with an established base of correspondents outside CGIAR.

The CBMS pilot study, and the extended network study, began in October 1983. The five research centres and the CGIAR and TAC secretariats comprised the initial users. During the study, two more centres were also brought on-line: the International Center for Tropical Agriculture (CIAT) in Cali, Colombia, and the International Potato Center (CIP) in Lima, Peru. Nine months later, an on-line survey of system users was conducted to determine how well they thought the system was working. The data presented in the following paragraphs summarize the results of that survey. The results were calculated using percentages to give equal weight to the responses of each centre. (If the number of respondents had been used, the analysis would have favoured centres in which more people responded.)

Most centres were satisfied with the CBMS. Respondents rated the pilot application of the CBMS on a 5-point scale ranging from "1 — very unsuccessful" to "5 — completely successful." The mean response was 3.5, which meant that most of the centres felt the CBMS pilot fell between the categories "somewhat successful" and "successful." Some of the centres that rated the CBMS as only "somewhat successful" qualified their responses with the comments that the system had not yet been used to its capacity and that it was still too limited because there were too few locations on the network. All of the centres felt that the CBMS should be continued. Comments ranged from "should and must" be continued to "emphatic recommendation."

The majority of CBMS usage (80%) was for administrative purposes. Seventy-five percent of the centres used the system to obtain or transmit travel information and 63% used it to obtain information for coordinating meetings. Fifty percent of the centres used the system to obtain financial information, especially for price quotes and purchasing. Transfers of scientific data accounted for 20% of the message traffic and consisted mainly of technical, computer-oriented information. Of the scientific-data traffic, specific requests for information on equipment and on database access each amounted to 13%.

The centres were asked: "If the CBMS project were to be continued, do you have any suggestions as to what the major emphases should be?" They responded with a wide variety of suggestions. Major emphasis was placed on

- Getting the remaining centres on-line and expanding the network;

- Supporting and promoting both CBMS and general office automation; and

- Training to ensure effective use of the system and the equipment used for accessing the network.

CBMS System Usage and Cost Effectiveness

Initial CBMS system usage in the pilot project totalled about 10 hours in January 1984, but rose to 81 hours in September 1984. From September until the end of 1984, usage levelled off at about 90 hours per month. Usage then started rising and reached 140 hours by May 1985.

At that time, the CBMS was already considered a worthwhile and cost-effective means of communication for CGIAR. The design for the system required no centralized equipment purchases, no major capital expenditures (that is, less than 2 500 USD per centre was required for the pilot), no centralized CGIAR facility, and no additional central staffing. The capabilities of the system were not subject to early obsolescence because the system relied on services rather than on equipment acquisition. Additionally, future migration to new services was an option that would require minimal effort.

To assess what steps to take next, a cost model was constructed in 1985, which estimated the cost of interconnecting all 15 sites (the nine centres that were already using CBMS through data networks and the six centres not currently on the CBMS). International direct dial (IDD) calls and other access alternatives were considered. For the sites not currently on the CBMS, the cost of 10 hours of international telephone calls per month (at 2.50 USD per minute) was included. The model assumed that 2 000 USD would be spent for equipment (high-quality modems) for the 15 centres (amortized over 5 years) and that equipment would be replaced in 1989.

Expansion of the system permitted a considerable cost savings for CGIAR, compared with its previous mode of operation (Table 1). Estimates of the displacement of communication costs and of the net impact were made. CGIAR stood to save several hundred thousand

Table 1. CBMS cost impact (millions of USD).

| Year | PMO[a] | DISP[b] | CBMS expense | | | | | Impact |
			IDD	Usage	Equipment	PTT	Total	
1984	1.983	0.456	0.108	0.015	0.006	0.011	0.140	−0.316
1985	2.241	0.515	0.122	0.017	0.006	0.012	0.157	−0.358
1986	2.532	0.582	0.138	0.019	0.006	0.014	0.177	−0.406
1987	2.861	0.658	0.156	0.022	0.006	0.016	0.199	−0.459
1988	3.233	0.744	0.176	0.024	0.006	0.018	0.224	−0.519
1989	3.654	0.840	0.199	0.028	0.006	0.020	0.253	−0.588
1990	4.129	0.950	0.225	0.031	0.006	0.022	0.285	−0.665
Total	20.632	4.745	1.124	0.156	0.042	0.112	1.434	−3.311

Note: See Acronyms and Abbreviations for definitions.
[a] Previous mode of operation, 13% annual growth.
[b] Communication cost displacement by CBMS, 23%.

dollars each year. The cumulative impact was projected to be over 3 million USD saved by 1990.

Cost models were also developed based on more and less conservative estimates. In the most conservative case (assuming a 7% annual increase in traditional communications costs and a 13% displacement), CBMS usage still offered savings of 1 million USD compared with the cost of the previous mode of communication. The most optimistic case (assuming a 13% annual increase in communication costs and a 35% displacement) showed savings for CGIAR of close to 6 million USD by 1990.

The "bottom line" of this exercise was that CGIAR stood to save millions of dollars by using the CBMS in place of existing methods of communication. Even greater savings could be obtained if agricultural researchers outside CGIAR were included. Surveys of the CGIAR centres revealed that a substantial proportion of their communication was with universities and other research centres. This finding suggested that a broader definition of the agricultural research community was appropriate. Although savings from intercentre communication alone would have been substantial, linking others in the agricultural research community to the network offered the possibility of tremendous savings on communication costs. A third potential source of cost savings was decreased travel expenses. CBMS was expected to decrease the need for travel by allowing rapid and reliable communication among far-flung centres. To give an example: if only 5% of travel were avoided by using CBMS, an additional 3.5 million USD would have been saved during this period.

After reviewing these figures, CGIAR began efforts to get the remaining "hard-to-reach" centres on-line. At the same time, many other centres, including some outside CGIAR, were invited to join the network.

Since the 1985 study, there has been no additional formal cost-effectiveness study. By 1992, some 25 000 pages of text were moving each month in and out of the network. It is certainly safe to say that if this traffic were moved by telex or facsimile, the costs would be much higher. On the other hand, the introduction of the technology introduced changes in communication patterns. The 1985 study required about 1 year to complete and was well funded. To redo this type of analysis would require a significant amount of effort and is beyond the scope of this book. However, the assumptions have generally held, except that adoption and usage grew much faster than predicted.

The initial large cost savings resulted from the substitution of · e-mail for telex (and in some cases telegrams). Now that almost all sites are connected to the e-mail network, dramatic costs savings are more difficult to find. Nonetheless, CGNET staff regularly evaluate options for further cost reductions (such as least-cost routing of telexes and facsimiles).

CGNET Services International

As this network, which had become known as "CGNET," expanded, so did the need for network administration. After some deliberation, the CGIAR Secretariat decided, in 1985, that it would prefer not to administer the network itself. The consulting company that did the original pilot study and model (Telematics International) was not interested in providing a continuing service operation. One of the Telematics consultants offered to administer CGNET and formed the company CGNET Services International (CSI) for that purpose. Among the functions CSI performed were purchasing CBMS computer equipment and service in bulk, billing individual users for network service, and maintaining the network directory. CSI also provided training and troubleshooting assistance, including consulting visits when appropriate. To cover the costs of these services, CSI charged network membership fees.

This arrangement proved satisfactory to CGIAR because it offered cost savings and helped encourage network growth. No additional expenditures on overhead were required from the CGIAR Secretariat because all network costs were charged to the users. Administration by a private company was also considered more likely to encourage the growth of the network to serve the entire agricultural research community. The CGIAR Secretariat feared that the system would remain limited to the CGIAR centres if it administered the system

itself. This would be counterproductive given the frequent communication of the centres with researchers outside the CGIAR system.

Because many of the network users were in countries that had
no previous experience with data communication, consultants from
CSI were often asked to get centres on-line. In many cases, this meant
assisting with the establishment of microwave and satellite links,
running a dial-out operation, and procuring computer and communication equipment that was either unavailable locally or too expensive to be purchased locally.

Growth in Members and Services

Since 1985, the network has grown steadily. All but two of the
"difficult-to-reach" centres were on-line by the end of 1986. When
other research centres joined the network during 1987, there were
more than 100 mailboxes in use in 18 countries. Many centres also
brought their regional offices on-line, which accounted for a large
part of the growth of the network during late 1987 and 1988. In late
1988 and 1989, several of the non-CGIAR IARCs joined the network,
including the Asian Vegetable Research and Development Center
(AVRDC) in Taipei, Taiwan, the International Board for Soil Research
and Management (IBSRAM) in Bangkok, the International Center for
Living Aquatic Resources Management (ICLARM) in Manila, the
International Center for Research in Agroforestry (ICRAF) in Nairobi,
and the International Irrigation Management Institute (IIMI) in
Colombo, Sri Lanka. By early 1992, some 490 mailboxes were in use
in 61 countries (a list of users by country is given in Appendix 2).

From 1987 to March 1992, 45 to 50 mailboxes were added each
year (Fig. 1). Because of the introduction of CGNET II in April 1992
(see pp. 27, 32–33), the number of mailboxes increased more than
fourfold, reaching 1 552 by December 1992. As of the end of August
1993, there was a total of 2 011 mailboxes. However, despite the
steady increase in the number of mailboxes on the network, a few of
the initial users did not stay on the network. This usually occurred
when individuals in large organizations opened e-mail accounts, but
use of CGNET did not become institutionalized. For example,

individuals in a few prominent donor and government technical assistance organizations started to use the network and then withdrew, such as at the Canadian International Development Agency (CIDA), the German Agency for Technical Cooperation (GTZ), and the Technical Centre for Agricultural and Rural Cooperation (CTA) in the Netherlands. Unlike in comparable organizations (such as the Australian International Development Assistance Bureau (AIDAB), the Australian Centre for International Agricultural Research (ACIAR), and IDRC), in which usage of CGNET spread throughout the institution, the CGNET mailboxes at CIDA, CTA, and GTZ were personal e-mail boxes belonging to a few individual staff members. Instead of increasing their e-mail communications, one or two of these former users have chosen in recent years to adopt facsimile for their international communication. The other "disconnections" generally took place when a particular person left the location, or took an extended leave, and the network service was left idle. In all of these cases, network usage was limited to one or two people in each organization rather than becoming institutionalized.

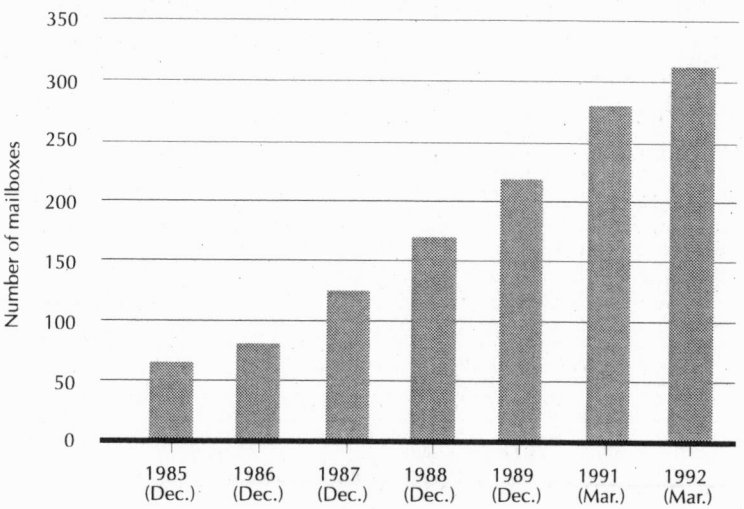

Fig. 1. Growth in number of CGNET mailboxes
(December 1985 to March 1992).

The large majority of current CGNET users, however, have stayed on-line. This has especially been the case with agricultural researchers because CGNET contains a "critical mass" of colleagues with whom frequent communication is important.

The movement of personnel within and between agricultural research institutions helped to spread the network more widely. For example, one researcher who was transferred from his institute's Bangkok office to its Harare office made sure that Harare was brought on-line after he arrived. In another case, an administrator moved from an institute in Niger to another in Sri Lanka and brought along the use of CGNET. Movement among centres continues to increase the growth of CGNET, especially when researchers accustomed to using the network move from headquarters to branch offices.

As the number of users grew, an increasing variety of services were provided on the network. In addition to sending regular e-mail messages, CGNET users were soon able to send telex and facsimile messages over the network. This allowed them to communicate with scientists and researchers at locations that had no e-mail. "Refiling" of telex and facsimile messages sent over the network has been particularly advantageous for researchers attempting to reach colleagues in countries with overloaded telecommunications systems. If messages are undeliverable, the system stores them and attempts to "refile" them another time, which saves the user the trouble of trying again and again.

Among the newest services are links to the developed-country academic networks, like BITNET and EARN (the European Academic Research Network), and access to on-line databases. The links to the academic networks have facilitated electronic correspondence with colleagues at hundreds of universities. Some members of CGNET have also begun to use special services, including public databases and news-wire services, that can be searched while on-line to the network. Usage of the system doubled and then doubled again (Fig. 2).

Notably, much of this growth in usage resulted from more intensive use of the network per unit of time. Starting in 1987, many

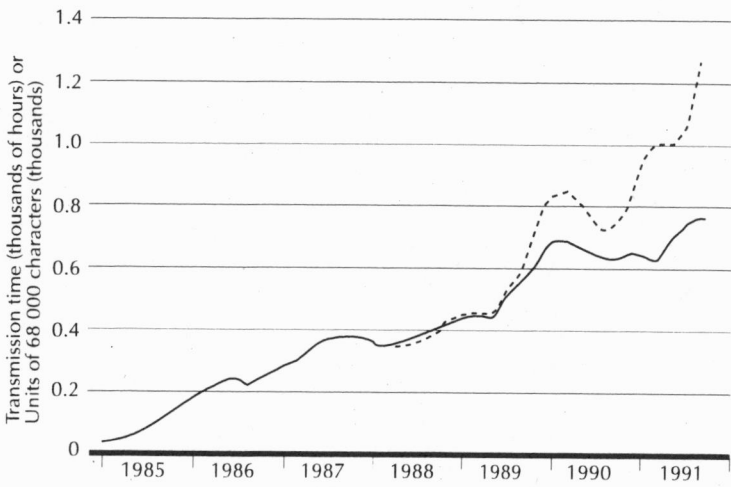

Fig. 2. CBMS usage expressed as hours of transmission time (solid line) and as units of 68 000 characters (dashed line) sent and received by the CGNET member organizations.

users upgraded their equipment to double their transmission speed (changing from modems that transmit 120 characters per second to those that send 240 characters per second). In addition, users sent more and longer messages during each network connection, which further increased the average character count per unit of time.

Figure 2 compares the growth of network use in terms of time and volume of messages. Since data became available in 1987, the number of characters passing through the system has grown even more quickly than the hours of use. Because the cost of the system for most users varies significantly by time as well as by volume, greater cost efficiencies have been realized as the network has grown.

Chapter 2

CGNET TODAY: HOW IT WORKS

CGNET is now used from more than 200 locations in over 60 countries (Fig. 3). This chapter describes the network's basic services, looks at methods used to connect to the network, and presents three organizational models used to integrate network facilities into centre operations.

CGNET provides a number of information and message-transfer services. Originally, CGNET did not maintain its own physical telecommunications system, instead using those provided by British Telecom, BT Tymnet, Cable and Wireless, Mercury Communication, Kenya Post and Telecom, and the Bay Area Regional Research Network. Now, computer and communication gateway facilities are maintained at the Menlo Park headquarters of CGNET Services International.

Basic Functions

The single most important function of the CGNET system is to provide e-mail for its users. An e-mail box can be thought of as a place where users both deposit and pick up their mail. Although this e-mail function is similar to telex and facsimile systems in that it provides a way to move messages from one place to another, it differs significantly because of its mailbox structure. The most basic difference is that users are not attached to the network on a permanent basis, as they are with telex and facsimile. CGNET members connect to the network periodically, using a computer and a telephone line, much

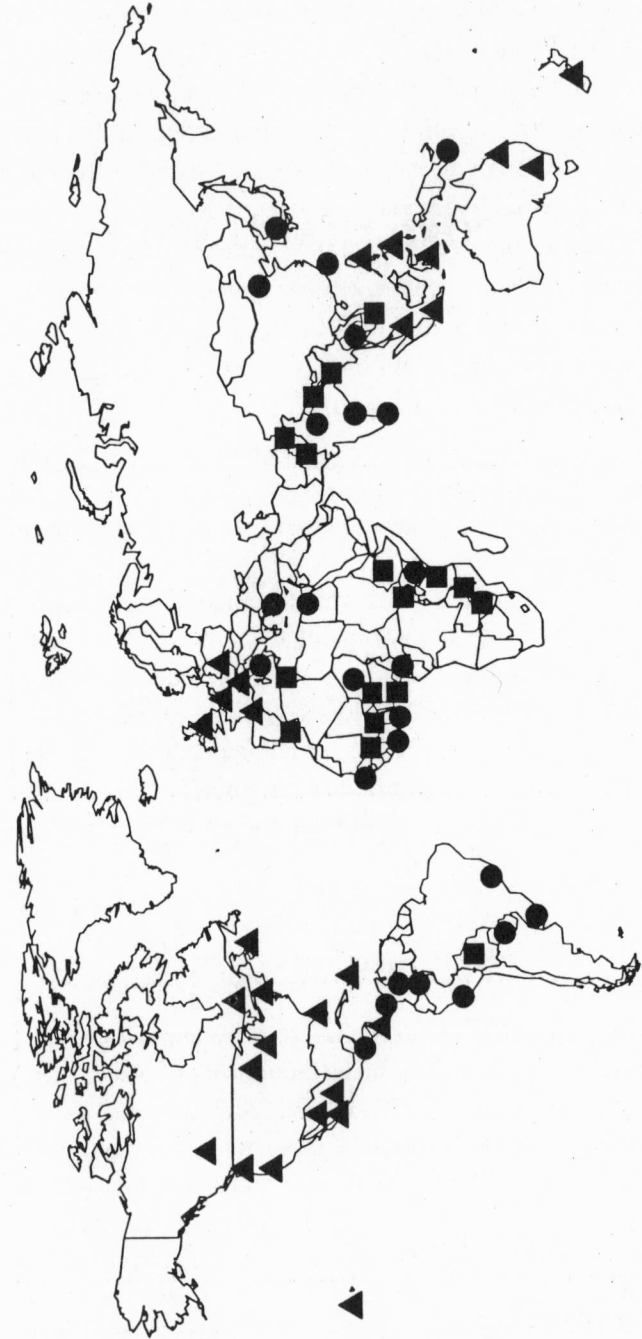

Fig. 3. Locations of CGNET mailboxes and modes of access: ▲, inexpensive national data networks; ●, other national data networks; ■, international direct dial location.

as a person with an ordinary post office box goes to the post office periodically to get mail.

Therefore, to the user, the CGNET system appears as a electronic depot for mail, with a "pigeon-hole" for each user (Fig. 4). To CGNET users, it seems as though all the mailboxes are located in the same place, and all are equally accessible. In fact, CGNET mailboxes are kept in a number of physically separate computers that are linked in a way that makes them appear to be one system. These computers are located in the United States, the United Kingdom, and several other countries. Depending on the needs of the user, a mailbox may be located in any of these countries.

IFPRI	WARDA	IRRI	ISNAR	ILRAD
CIMMYT	ILCA	IBSRAM	CGIAR Secretariat	TAC Secretariat
CIP	CIAT	USAID	Pudoc	IIMI
ACIAR	IBPGR	ICRISAT	UNDP	CABI

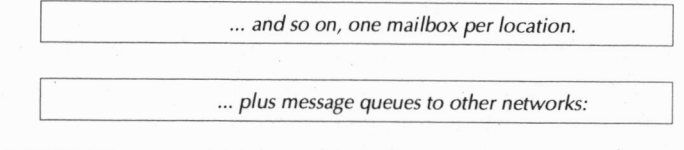

... and so on, one mailbox per location.

... plus message queues to other networks:

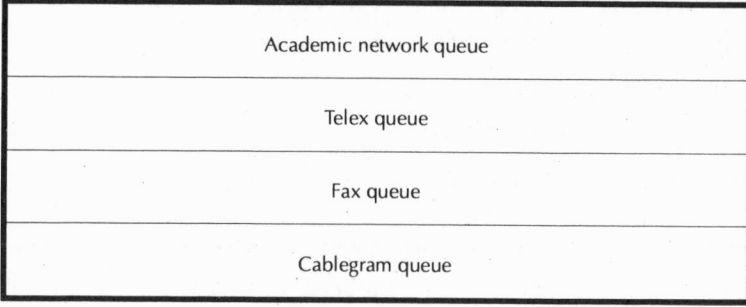

Academic network queue

Telex queue

Fax queue

Cablegram queue

Fig. 4. Representation of CGNET system mailboxes and queues.

To use the e-mail facility, users send a message to the CGNET computer, which then copies the message into the recipient's electronic mailbox. If the message is intended for more than one mailbox, the user still sends it just once. The system will copy it into each recipient's mailbox, automatically and instantly. This ability to distribute messages to several addresses at once is one of the inherent advantages of an e-mail system.

CGNET also provides a telex, facsimile, and cablegram refiling function. Messages are sent to a queue, where they are held for delivery to telex or facsimile machines worldwide, or to international cablegram services. If the telex or facsimile machine is busy, the system will requeue the messages and try again later. In addition, each mailbox is assigned a telex number, and telexes sent to this number are automatically stored in the mailbox, exactly like incoming e-mail messages. A user's mailbox can, therefore, completely replace a telex machine, both for sending and receiving telexes.

Finally, the system contains several referral features that transport messages to and from developed-country academic e-mail networks such as BITNET, EARN, JANET, and NetNorth. As in the case of telexes and facsimiles, this "gateway" is a mailbox where messages can be deposited for retransmission to these other networks. These gateways to the commercial message services and the academic networks are extremely important because they allow CGNET users to communicate with others who do not have access to CGNET. These academic gateways also dramatically increase the reach of CGNET, because more than 6 million people exchange e-mail on the academic networks. Many of the researchers in the centres can now correspond by e-mail with their colleagues, collaborators, and advisors at these institutions.

Enhanced Functions

At a 1989 meeting of the computer heads of many CGIAR centres, strong support was given to a proposal to establish a new set of e-mail services. The proposal called for CGNET to provide enhanced mail services to institutions that had developed internal data networks and to provide a better link to the academic networks. The recommendations from this conference became the charter to develop CGNET II — the next evolutionary step for the network.

The original CGNET was implemented at isolated institutions in an attempt to replace telex and telegram communications; however, CGNET II was designed to extend e-mail services from centralized communication rooms directly to scientists' desktops. It was built on the internal electronic data networks that were available at many of the centres. These local area networks (LANs) already connected users' personal computers to each other and normally supported internal e-mail systems.

Using a conventional CBMS (like the original CGNET), a network member would connect to a central mailbox that served the entire organization; mail that arrived at the central mailbox was then distributed internally, often by hand. By connecting the LANs to the CGNET II service, subscribers obtained a system-to-system link, in which incoming mail was routed automatically to each user's internal mailbox. Most mail could be transferred without any operator intervention and, therefore, passed from the desktop computer of the sender, through various automatic links, to the desktop computer of the recipient. The implications of this "desk-to-desk" e-mail transfer are examined in more detail later in this chapter.

Connection Methods

To pick up and drop off messages, CGNET users must connect their computers to the network. More precisely, a connection must be established between the user's computer system and the computer in CGNET that contains the user's electronic mailbox. For simplicity, the computer containing the mailbox will be called "the CGNET computer."

The connection to the CGNET computer is actually the end product of three different connections:

➤ The user's computer must be physically connected (plugged in) to a device called a modem that must be wired, like an extension telephone, into the user's telephone line.

→ The user's computer must instruct the modem to connect to a data network node. In most cases, this requires an ordinary telephone call. (At a few centres, a computer with a permanent connection to a data network node has been installed using a modem on a dedicated telephone line. This eliminates the need to make a telephone call.) A network node is itself a specially programmed computer that has high-speed communication channels to other computers around the world, including the CGNET computer. The technical term for these data networks is "packet switching systems."

→ The user's computer must instruct the data network to connect it to the CGNET computer. From then on, the data network will relay anything sent by the user's computer to CGNET, and vice versa.

The result of this three-step process is that subscribers can use their computer's keyboard and screen to carry on a written conversation with CGNET and to send and receive messages or other information. Files of text or computer data can also be sent between CGNET and the user's computer. The user finishes this "conversation" by telling CGNET to terminate the data-network connection and by instructing the modem to "hang up" the telephone.

The cost and convenience of this process depend on the location from which one calls. In Figure 3, three methods of connection are shown. A fourth method, Inbound IDD, was used but is not now in use on CGNET.

→ **Inexpensive National Data Networks**: Institutions in some locations make local telephone calls to very inexpensive data-network services. These locations are typically in developed countries or in the capital cities of some developing countries (such as Mexico City). The cost of e-mail communication from these places ranges from 0.20 to 0.50 USD for a full page of text (about 2 000 characters). Because only high-quality local telephone calls are made, inexpensive modems can be used. These modems are available at a cost of from 60 to 150 USD.

➤ **Other National Data Networks**: In some countries, calling a national data network is expensive, either because the data network has set high charges, or because the user must place a long-distance call to reach the network. The total cost per page ranges from 0.50 to 1.00 USD. In these locations, an error-correcting modem that can compensate for noisy telephone lines is preferable. These modems cost 200 USD or more.

➤ **International Direct Dial** (IDD): In countries that do not have national data networks, users must dial a data network in another country. International calls tend to be quite expensive; therefore, per-page costs rise to as high as 2.00 USD. In addition, wasted time during a connection costs a lot of money. Because every e-mail call includes some wasted time, an "overhead" cost (a cost in addition to the cost of transferring data) must be anticipated. Overhead costs can run as high as 300 USD per month for those who connect using international calls. Finally, costs are also higher in these locations because high-quality, high-speed modems must be used. These modems cost about 600 USD. Because there are usually no local suppliers of error-correcting modems in these areas, users usually keep a second modem on hand as a backup, which further increases their initial costs.

➤ **Inbound IDD**: In a few special cases, international calls do not suffice. This situation occurs in countries where telephone lines cannot dial internationally or where national telephone systems are so overloaded that calls are very difficult to make. However, if these institutions can receive calls, their computers can be called and instructed to pick up and drop off mail. Because these calls must be made at night (when the local telephone system is least congested) the user's computer must be left on all night to receive the call. The extra administrative burden of sending and receiving e-mail this way is usually justified only when the user has a relatively large volume of messages to communicate. The only long-term user of this method has been the International Crops Research Institute for the Semi-Arid Tropics (ICRISAT), in Hyderabad, India, which used Inbound IDD from 1985 to 1989.

Table 2 provides sample costs for message transfers using the more common access methods. The charges include telephone costs, data-network costs, and mailbox costs. In each case, there are monthly charges for maintaining accounts, as well as charges proportional to the amount of message traffic sent through the system.

The costs presented in Table 2 are approximate. Costs vary a great deal and depend on how well the local telephone system works and how efficiently the system is used. For example, these estimates assume that the user prepares all messages before initiating a message transfer. If messages are prepared while the user is logged onto the system, the total cost would include connect time charges and would therefore be higher.

Another factor that influences cost is the time required to set up the connection and to prepare to send the messages. This time can be thought of as housekeeping or overhead time. The overhead in Table 2 represents the cost to log onto the system to check for mail twice each business day. Checking more often, or repeatedly calling because of telephone failures, increases overhead costs. The telephone connection is not typically a problem for users of nearby data networks, but it can generate additional overhead costs for IDD users.

No matter what assumptions are used, however, it is clear that costs vary greatly depending on how the system is accessed. Because

Table 2. Sample messaging costs (1992 USD).

	Data network		IDD	
	Low cost	High cost	Low cost	High cost
Monthly fees				
Mailbox	10	10	10	10
Data network	0	25	0	0
Overhead	20	50	150	350
Total	30	85	160	360
Usage costs (per page sent or received)				
Mailbox	0.18	0.18	0.18	0.18
Data network	0.03	0.80	0.00	0.20
Telephone	0.00	0.00	0.50	1.80
Total	0.21	0.98	0.68	2.18

Note: See Acronyms and Abbreviations for definitions.

the usage costs affect both incoming and outgoing messages, locations with high-cost or low-quality communication infrastructures pay much more for CBMS access. However, the costs for mailbox service account for a small proportion of the total cost of e-mail. The bulk of the costs results from the movement of data between the user and the mailbox service.

Styles of Interaction

After one of these four types of connection has been established, messages and data can be moved between a user's computer and CGNET. At this stage, there is yet another level of variation among users: the organizational environment that stands between the end-user and the communication link. There are three general models for an organization's interface to CGNET:

➤ **The Message Room Model**: In this model, a personal computer (PC) and a modem are placed in a central location, usually next to the existing telex or facsimile machine, and CGNET is treated as another centralized communication resource. A clerical person, often the telex operator, is designated as the e-mail operator. Users submit their outgoing messages to the operator on paper or on a floppy disk and they receive their incoming mail on paper. If computer data are received in a message, the data are transferred from the message room PC to the user's computer, usually on a floppy disk. The message room model is easy to implement in most larger organizations, and it delivers most of the speed and economic benefits of the network with a minimum amount of training and reorganization.

➤ **The Solitary On-Line Model**: In this model, most professionals in the organization have their own mailboxes, and they (or their secretaries) check their boxes regularly. This model provides more responsive access, because the user need not rely on an operator to send a message or to check if a reply has arrived. It is also more confidential than the message room model because only the recipient sees the messages. For a solitary representative scientist posted overseas, this type of access can be especially valuable. However, this style of network interaction requires the user to have greater familiarity with computers. In addition, it can be more costly to operate if several professionals at one location have individual mailboxes (especially if they are located in a country where communication costs are high). Among CGNET users, CIAT, ICLARM, ISNAR, the Ford Foundation, Foster Parents Plan International (PLAN), Winrock International, and the Cameroon Office of the International Institute of Tropical Agriculture (IITA) rely most on this model and maintain many separate mailboxes for individual staff members or research teams. At other institutes, this model is mainly used by professionals who want to keep in touch when they travel or work at home.

→ The "Desk-to-Desk" Model: Centres that have mainframe computer centres or PC-based LANs often have in-house e-mail systems. Starting in 1986, some centres modified their in-house systems to allow their users to send and receive CGNET messages (including telex, facsimile, and regular e-mail messages) in the same way they handled in-house messages. In these systems, a special program is run every hour or two to connect to CGNET and transfer all of the centre's e-mail. Because the transfer is automatic, confidentiality is maintained, message transfers take place at predictable times, and communication can be very cost effective. Computer training can be greatly simplified when electronic "campus mail," long-distance e-mail, telex, facsimile, and other forms of data transfer all make use of a common user interface. CIMMYT, ICRISAT, and IRRI programmed their VAX minicomputers to operate this way before CGNET II was implemented. A few centres went half-way toward the "desk-to-desk" model by using an in-house e-mail system for outgoing CGNET messages and delivering incoming mail on paper (for example, CIP uses its VAXes and ISNAR has used its Wang computer system only for sending outgoing e-mail messages).

All these centres, and several others, either have adopted or are in the process of adopting the CGNET II service to achieve automatic two-way transfers. This change is part of a widespread trend in the international agricultural research community. Between 1983 and 1988, many more individuals were served by the message room model than by either the solitary on-line model or the desk-to-desk model. From 1989 and 1991, many solitary on-line users joined the network, especially at locations away from centre headquarters. At the same time, a few centres developed their own desk-to-desk methods; therefore, the balance between the models became more even. The growth in desk-to-desk users has been very rapid, and these users are now a majority in the CGNET community. Clearly, no single messaging model is best in all situations, but the growth in use of the desk-to-desk model demands further explanation of its structure and benefits.

Desk-to-Desk Messaging

"Desk-to-desk" message transfer can be compared to a Private Branch Exchange (PBX) office telephone system. In the same way that a PBX can automatically route incoming telephone calls to an extension telephone based on the original telephone number, desk-to-desk e-mail relies on a computer program to route messages to users' e-mail destinations, based on each individual's mailbox address. Just as a PBX can replace a human telephone operator, the desk-to-desk programs can replace the e-mail operator. The benefits are similar: with automatic switching, confidentiality is increased, and users experience a direct, immediate, and private connection.

To adopt desk-to-desk messaging, a centre must operate an internal e-mail system and must run a program that will transfer messages between the internal e-mail system and the CGNET II computer. This transfer program exchanges messages with CGNET II under the computer protocol in use at that centre. CGNET II supports a number of different protocols (including Microsoft Mail and X.400) to allow easy integration with the computer systems in use at different centres. It is the job of the CGNET II computer to relay messages on to their destinations, under whatever protocol is required (Fig. 5).

The CGNET II service also provides a direct connection to the academic networks, rather than just a gateway. This has simplified message exchange. Unlike other CGNET users, CGNET II clients do not have to provide special forwarding information when they address messages to the academic networks. Instead, they can use Internet-standard addresses to send messages to these correspondents. The delays imposed by the previous gateway operation are also

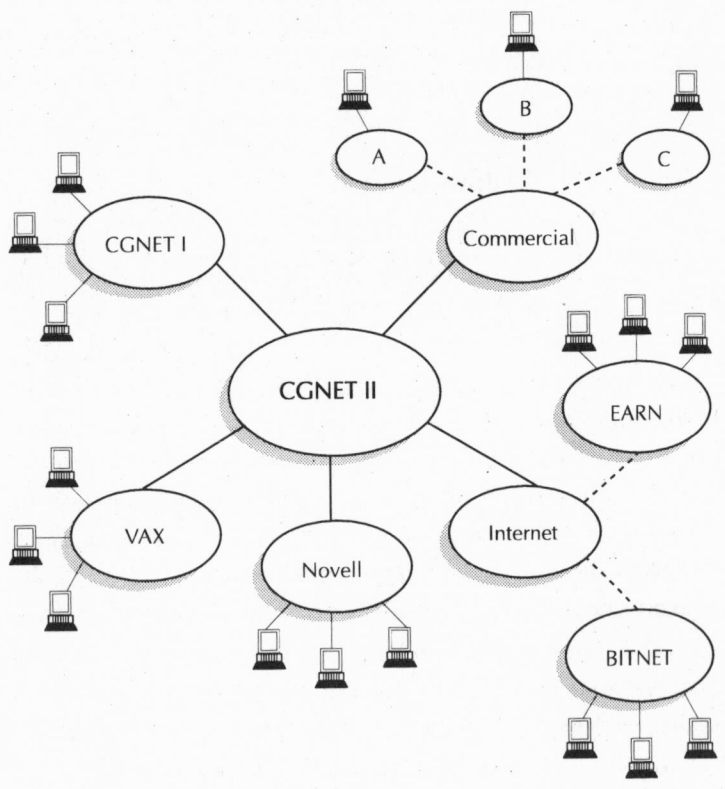

Fig. 5. Representation of CGNET internetworking, including VAX- and Novell-based centre LANs (solid lines represent direct connections; dashed lines, indirect connections).

eliminated. The result is that the users are essentially on the academic networks themselves.

The key to the successful integration of academic, commercial, and centre-based desk-to-desk networks is the directory service and software integration provided by the new CGNET II minicomputer. Communication links themselves are of limited usefulness without mechanisms that standardize addressing for the network. CGNET users can send mail to CGNET II destinations using exactly the same procedures they have always used, and correspondents on the Internet can address messages in their usual format. For example, a university professor on the Internet at the University of Houston could easily send a message to a colleague at the University of Florida with a copy to a CGNET subscriber at IRRI in the Philippines. The following format would be used:

> To: ghobbes@ag.fla.edu   (colleague in Florida)
> cc: j.rich@cgnet.com   (colleague in the Philippines)

In response, J. Rich could forward this message to a scientist down the hall with a few short commands. At the same time, the message could be easily forwarded to associates at IDRC in Canada and ICRISAT in India:

> MAILforward
> To: jgomez, k.jackson-idrc@cgnet.com,   (associates in Canada)
>   s.vishnu@cgnet.com   (associate in India)

Simplified addressing and direct lines to the academic networks have greatly increased the use of the system. For example, message traffic has doubled at IRRI since the introduction of desk-to-desk e-mail. ISNAR and ICRISAT have also seen an increase in e-mail use.

Along with the end-user benefits of desk-to-desk messaging come benefits for the institutions as well. Training for e-mail users is greatly simplified when the internal e-mail system can also be used to reach all other e-mail, telex, or facsimile correspondents. Costs are frequently reduced because telecommunication lines can be used more efficiently. Simpler and faster message transfer with the academic networks encourages closer collaboration with a wider variety of institutions. At IRRI in 1992, for example, a biotechnology question arose that was expected to take several months of research to resolve. By posting an e-mail question to a number of biotechnology researchers on the Internet, IRRI located an institution that had already found the answer to the question. A single exchange of messages with institutions outside CGIAR saved months of work and thousands of dollars.

Chapter 3

APPLICATIONS AND RESULTS

CGNET forms an information infrastructure for the agricultural research community, and like a road or a telephone, it supports many different uses. Although no formal survey has been conducted on usage, anecdotal user experience provides some basis for generalization.

Basic Messaging

Most of the data traffic passing over the network consists of messages, and many of these messages are administrative. Meetings are planned, trips arranged, budgets changed and reviewed, tasks proposed and authorized, publications announced and ordered, germplasm deliveries scheduled and confirmed, and purchases specified and approved. Much of this message traffic would have occurred by other means in the absence of the network, although generally with less detail and at much higher cost. A qualitative difference that e-mail users frequently report is that opinions and options are now much more detailed. E-mail messages are longer than telexes; therefore, they convey more information and allow more complete explanations. E-mail messages resemble memoranda, although they are more informal because they have neither a letterhead nor written signature.

CGNET e-mail messages play a large role in the internal administration of several CGIAR centres. Over the last few years, agricultural research has become more decentralized, as attempts have been made to adapt crops to more diverse environments and to involve local researchers more closely in the research. Establishment of research subcentres and increased postings of scientists to branch offices and research stations have greatly expanded the communication needs of the CGIAR system. Administrative communications that would have stayed at one location in the past are now circulated frequently among many locations using CGNET. Newsletters, policy memos, and other administrative publications can be circulated cheaply, and the ease of using the forwarding and editing functions has encouraged widespread circulation of administrative communications.

In every industry and university community where e-mail has been introduced, networks have made it easier for correspondents in distant locations to keep in touch. The CGNET community is no exception. People who meet at a conference might not mail letters or send expensive telexes to maintain contact, but they sometimes do use e-mail. Recent graduates or scientists returning from sabbatical also maintain contact with their home institutions using quick e-mail notes. Travellers pass their itinerary to many more people when this takes only a single e-mail message. Some users report that one of the best parts about the network is that, despite being stationed far from home in a place that is difficult to contact, they still feel that they are part of the broader research community.

Special Applications and Case Histories

In addition to the basic messaging functions of CGNET, a number of users have found special ways to take advantage of the network.

Experimental data collection and collaboration

Much of the scientific work in CGIAR consists of field trials of crops and agricultural techniques that are often conducted far from a research centre. Traditionally, data are noted by hand in field books, and the field books are sent back to the centre for analysis. The recent trend, however, is to perform preliminary data analysis in the field using small portable computers. Field data and preliminary analyses are now sent frequently through CGNET so that further analysis can be undertaken at the research centres.

For example, in one project at CIMMYT, a collaborator in the Middle East is studying the progress of a wheat disease called *Septoria*. His field books pass instantly over CGNET to researchers at CIMMYT headquarters for simultaneous analysis. Similarly, data on sorghum and millet trials flow on a regular basis from the ICRISAT Sahelian Centre in Niamey, Niger, to ICRISAT in Hyderabad, India, and are sometimes also sent to the University of Nottingham. At IRRI and other centres, data flow in both directions. Biotechnology data collected at Cornell University are sent over the network for analysis at IRRI, and vice versa. The main advantage of this type of simultaneous data analysis is that it allows immediate monitoring of results and feedback into subsequent experimental designs. E-mail can also provide valuable continuity on projects that continue after a visiting scientist has left a centre, allowing continued contact with that scientist.

With the addition of the CGNET gateway to Internet, a new type of collaboration began to develop. CGNET is now frequently used to seek advice from experts on Internet, sometimes by direct communication with one or two researchers, and sometimes by posting an inquiry to a large discussion group in one area of interest. For biotechnology researchers at IRRI, e-mail collaboration with experts on Internet has prevented unnecessary duplication of research and saved months of work. Collaborative problem solving and simultaneous data analysis have both increased the efficiency of the research process.

Production of joint reports and papers

When communication is fast and inexpensive, it becomes increasingly attractive to send reports for review before they are formally issued and to pass successive drafts of papers between authors. For example, two of the authors of this book used CGNET to coauthor a paper for a conference. One author was in California, and then travelled to Washington; the other was in Australia. Each author revised a draft and then passed it by e-mail to the other. Because of the time difference between the United States and Australia, 10 drafts were composed in 1 week. One author worked while the other slept. Thanks to e-mail, the two authors could work from the same draft and only needed to input their revisions. Thus, the e-mail system made collaboration easier and prevented duplication of effort. Another example of this process was the production of a statement of purpose and an agenda for an information conference. Contributions and suggestions were received from a number of centres, including CIAT in Colombia, CIMMYT in Mexico, CIP in Peru, IBPGR in Italy, ICRISAT in India, IFPRI in the United States, the International Livestock Centre for Africa (ILCA) in Ethiopia, and IRRI in the Philippines. After each suggestion was addressed, a new draft of the agenda was sent to each centre for further revision.

Although e-mail can facilitate collaboration on papers or other documents, this is a complex process on the Dialcom system. It is easy to move the text component of a document across the network, even between machines and word processors of different types. However, the formatting of the document will not be retained unless the authors make use of special software designed to transfer formatted documents. This complex method generally is not used for transfers of early drafts of most types of documents because the text is important, formatting is not.

However, some organizations have found it worthwhile to use additional software at each location to ensure that formatted documents can be moved among their different offices. The consulting group RTI (Research Triangle Institute), for example, moves drafts of formatted consultancy reports between its headquarters in North Carolina and its overseas sites. Biotechnology researchers at IRRI also make regular use of file-transfer software. One scientist has used the system to coauthor several papers with a collaborator at Cornell University. Two other biotechnology researchers make use of special file-transfer software to write joint papers with collaborators in other parts of the world. Another CGIAR scientist, who is responsible for administering a large Dutch project, uses CGNET to send formatted funding proposals and status reports to donor agencies in the Netherlands.

Questionnaire and report distribution

One of the central advantages of a CBMS is that it is easy and inexpensive to send messages to several locations at once because the message only needs to be sent once. If a list of addresses is provided, the mailbox computer will copy the message into each of the listed mailboxes. A very common use of this capability is the distribution of administrative questionnaires. For example, when administrators at ICLARM reviewed their compensation policy in 1988, they wanted to know how much other comparable institutions paid their staff. A single e-mail message took the place of eight telexes and thereby resulted in considerable cost savings.

Reports are also frequently distributed this way. Soon after getting on-line in 1988, IIMI prepared a report for distribution to 10 other institutions. Six of them were on CGNET. This allowed the 40-page report to be sent once, in 8 minutes, to all their mailboxes. (Of course, each recipient had to pick up the report, which took each of them from 2 to 8 minutes.) The other four copies had to be sent individually by facsimile, which took much longer and cost significantly more. Each facsimile transmission from Sri Lanka took over 30 minutes, and several of the international calls had to be tried repeatedly because of frequent disconnections.

Using news collections

A number of commercial databases are linked to the CGNET system. Several popular databases contain collections of news stories maintained by the major wire services. One service provided on the network scans items as they are added to the news database. If a news item matches a profile specified by a user, the item is automatically placed in the user's mailbox. CIMMYT obtains the monthly figures of the United States Department of Agriculture (USDA) on wheat rust statistics this way. The news service also provides ICRISAT with an accurate daily report of world exchange rates, information that can be difficult to obtain in Hyderabad, India. In times of crisis, the news wires become particularly valuable. For example, after the earthquake in Mexico and during the Gulf War, there was a definite increase in use of the news services. In addition to concern for the well-being of the centre personnel, there were practical considerations such as whether travel should proceed or be cancelled, whether workshops should take place, and whether meetings should be rescheduled.

Ordering and publicizing books

Publications and library departments of the CGIAR institutes are also heavy users of CGNET. The network is frequently used to convey press releases, book orders, shipping information, and loan requests. When one centre publishes a book, it sends announcements to other centres. The book is ordered over the network, and the shipping information is sent back over the network when the book is dispatched. CGNET users can also reach other suppliers and publishers who are on-line. Elsevier Science Publishers in Holland will rush-order books in response to an e-mail message, and any company with telex, facsimile, or e-mail equipment can easily be reached through CGNET. In addition, ICRISAT's Union Catalog of Serials database, in use at many centres, can automatically generate inter-library loan requests that are transmitted over the network.

Message refiling

In most developing countries, telex, cable, and facsimile (telephone) rates are well above those in most developed countries. There are valid economic reasons behind the disparity in prices. If the rates in a country are higher, outgoing calls will be kept to a minimum and the number of incoming calls will be much higher than the number of outgoing calls. International telecommunications accounts are settled in such a way that the country that receives the most calls receives a payment (in hard currency) from the country that made the most calls. By setting high rates, telecommunications authorities can ensure themselves of an inflow of hard foreign currency. Consequently, most developing countries have more expensive international telecommunications services than developed countries, where foreign exchange issues are less important.

To circumvent this practice, large telecommunications users, such as banks and international corporations, often send their telex or facsimile messages over data networks that allow telexes and facsimiles to originate in countries with lower telecommunications prices. In this way, they significantly lower their costs. CGIAR centres follow the same procedure when using CGNET. Centres in developing countries send their telex and facsimile messages to the CGNET system, which then refiles them by transmitting them from the United States or the United Kingdom at their rates. Of the 12 CGIAR centres in developing countries, 6 refile the bulk of their messages this way and thus substantially reduce their communications costs. At a large centre, savings from telex and facsimile refiling can exceed 2 000 USD per month.

Refiling also eliminates the difficulty of trying to contact colleagues in countries with unreliable telex systems. Getting through to many African countries is often time consuming and frustrating. From ISNAR in the Netherlands, for example, it can take hours to complete a telex call to Rwanda. Sending a telex to Rwanda through CGNET is much easier: ISNAR sends the telex to CGNET, which automatically tries to deliver the telex every few minutes until it gets through.

Contact with advisory committees

A number of board members, chairpersons, and TAC members have personal mailboxes on CGNET. Establishing immediate and confidential contact with them can be extremely useful at critical times. For example, when the West Africa Rice Development Association (WARDA) first joined CGNET, its Director General needed to contact its Chairman twice daily to review preparations for an institutional review and to pass drafts of sensitive letters back and forth. Even under normal conditions, CGNET is very useful for the circulation of agendas and other materials in preparation for board meetings and program reviews. Agendas can be circulated quickly at low cost, and feedback can be provided within days. Similarly, documents and papers can be sent quickly, with none of the delays inherent to postal mail systems.

Contact with travellers and scientists on leave

An inherent advantage of e-mail systems is that they are independent of the location of the users. Network members can move from
place to place, and receive mail at each place, without having to
inform everyone of their itinerary. Some frequent travellers in the
CGIAR Secretariat use this facility regularly. Several centres also
maintain mailboxes to allow scientists who are on leave to maintain
contact. For example, IRRI used this method to stay in touch with an
economist spending a year at Harvard, and ICRISAT opened a box for
its Director General when he spent 3 months in Hawaii. Using this
system, a CIP scientist was able to check his mail from Mexico, the
United States, France, and Ethiopia during a recent home leave and
to maintain continuity in his experiments despite his distance from
them. At any given time, 10 to 20 CGNET mailboxes are in use for this
purpose.

World Bank gateway

The World Bank and the International Monetary Fund (IMF) have a
joint e-mail system for internal use that has over 5 000 personal
mailboxes. The system grew piecemeal over many years and has
many types of equipment, including IBM mainframes, DEC VAXes,
Wang word processors, and PC-based LANs. Several parts of the
organization had their own internal e-mail system. An internal
software gateway was purchased to unite these networks and, in
1987, CGNET was chosen to provide an external link. CGNET users can
now send messages to the personal mailbox of anyone at the World
Bank, and members of the Bank can reply directly from their desks
to CGNET users. The World Bank has now installed additional links
to parts of the United Nations system and has expanded its internal
connections.

Alternative telecommunications facilities

E-mail in any form requires some telecommunications link, usually
a telephone line. Other means are possible but rarely necessary if the
telephone works. Generally, every research location wants

functional telephones before it has e-mail. As a result, considerable effort has been made to improve the basic telecommunications facilities at several centres. The International Institute of Tropical Agriculture (IITA) and IRRI both built microwave towers to connect to the national grid in the capital city and circumvent problems with the local telephone systems. Both systems improved the ability of the centres to complete calls within the national capital. In addition, the IRRI installation helped provide reliable international telephone service. Unfortunately, the IITA microwave link has not provided reliable international telephone service. The difficulties experienced by IITA appear to be the result of problems with the national system rather than with the microwave link itself. These problems have made CGNET access difficult by conventional means.

Satellites provide another alternative link for centres located in areas with difficult communications. Satellite technology can be used to reach the network when civil unrest or other problems make the national telephone system completely unreliable. For example, IIMI chose to use a satellite dish when civil disturbances near their previous headquarters at Kandy, Sri Lanka, repeatedly disrupted the national telephone system. IIMI investigated several alternatives and installed an Inmarsat-based satellite dish early in 1989. Inmarsat devices function completely independently of local or national tele-communications systems; therefore, they overcome problems with unreliable local telecommunications links. Although satellite com-munication is expensive (about 10 USD per minute to any telephone in the world), it provided IIMI with a link when all other services failed. A similar system was installed at IITA in 1991. This system has allowed IITA to bypass the troublesome ground telephone system and ensure reliable access to CGNET.

Each of these alternative arrangements required careful coordi-nation with the national post, telephone, and telegraph organiza-tions (PTTs) because they were somewhat suspicious of equipment that bypassed the national telephone system. In the case of the microwave systems, the centres, in effect, paid for additions to the national telephone systems. Although IRRI and IITA were responsible for overseeing the construction and paying for the microwave towers, a condition of the approval was ownership by the national PTTs. In the case of the satellites, the equipment had to be registered with the PTTs.

Lesser Used Applications

Many applications were envisaged when CGNET was created; a few have never really been used (Appendix 1 lists applications from a 1983 survey of potential telecommunication uses).

Interactive on-line conferences

A "computer conference" is the electronic equivalent of a bulletin board: a place where messages can be left for any user to read at any time. Computer conferences allow written conversations to develop. One posted message responds to another, in a sequence that can become quite long and involved. Unlike a mailbox, whose contents are read by one user and then deleted, the contents of a conference are available to many users, and they accumulate over time. This allows new users to catch up on past contributions to the conference and even to search the proceedings for material that they find interesting. A computer conference can sometimes perform the function of a meeting by allowing a group to share their experiences. Conferences vary in structure from simple to very complex, depending on the needs of the group. Some conference systems are as simple as an ordinary bulletin board, with little structure. Others attempt to model the social processes of a meeting by allowing side comments among participants and by giving a "moderator" significant control over the agenda and proceedings.

Initially, conferences were not very popular with CGNET clients. Conferencing systems rely on each user having personal access to the system. However, this was not the case at most CGIAR centres. In the beginning, only one or two trained e-mail operators used CGNET. In addition, CGNET members were able to obtain many of the group communications functions of a conference by simply posting messages to a "distribution list" of mailboxes. All interested parties received each relevant message as soon as it was sent, and new members were simply sent copies of old messages to bring their correspondence records up to date.

This "distribution list" method was formalized on CGNET in 1990 as a "remote electronic meeting" or REM. An operating REM requires a mailbox to which messages can be sent, and a program that periodically compiles the messages in the mailbox and sends them to a distribution list. This resembles the "list servers" used on academic networks such as Internet and BITNET. REM proceedings are formatted for easy printing and filing and carry date and time stamps. These features allow users who do not have individual mailboxes to interact with the REM just as they would with an e-mail correspondent. There is no need to learn any special commands or procedures, or even to be personally on-line at all.

Although traditional interactive computer conferences were never widely used on CGNET, REMs have proven effective for working groups and special interest groups. Computer facility managers have had an ongoing REM for almost 3 years, and the organizers of a CGIAR information management conference used a REM to discuss the agenda and prepare the final list of participants. There are also REMs for librarians, public awareness task force members, and biodiversity working group members. Today, REMS are also under consideration for biotechnology researchers and geographic information specialists.

Database sharing

At first, it was thought that databases would be placed on CGNET to provide many kinds of information (such as policies, finances, and bibliographies). None have been established to date. The main reason is that the person who needs the information rarely operates the network link. Additionally, the high communication costs from many locations deter most users from browsing through an on-line database — or even learning how to use it.

The learning problem also deters widespread database use. In many centres, professionals rarely search existing campus-wide databases themselves. They prefer to ask for help from someone who knows how to use databases. These requests and resulting searches sometimes travel over the network as messages and provide remote professionals with much the same service they would get if they were on the centre campus. Because these researchers frequently choose not to conduct the searches themselves, there has been little demand for databases that are accessible over the network. In the future, other technologies, such as CD-ROM (compact disk — read-only memory), may provide a better way to disseminate databases to researchers. Not only do CD-ROMs hold a tremendous amount of information, when they are on-site, they overcome barriers such as cost that currently keep on-line database searching to a minimum (these issues are more fully discussed in Chapter 5). However, widespread use of databases over CGNET does not seem likely unless communication costs decrease or technology changes significantly.

Text translation

In principle, the network can be used to transport documents between authors and translators to facilitate translation into different languages. Centres in a Spanish-speaking area, for example, might help authors at other centres translate their writings for Spanish publication. Service companies specializing in translation might even offer translation as a paid service to other network clients. This has not happened on a widespread basis. One reason is a basic limitation in the technology and, indeed, in computer hardware in general. The most widely used computer character set, called ASCII, is designed around an English (or American) keyboard and does not include the characters of other languages. When these other characters are included, they are usually provided in a form unique to each type of computer. For example, the European characters of IBM mainframes do not match those of DEC, nor those of Wang or Data General (to say nothing of Japanese or other characters). This type of problem was described earlier with regard to word processors: each one shares minimal (ASCII) text capability, but no general standard is in force for formatting codes. The e-mail character set is superior to that of telex, and additional software will perform the necessary character conversions for users. But, to date, non-English characters are not fully supported by all users on the network and, therefore, they are rarely used.

In addition, automatic translation systems have drawn attention among translators. This is a different kind of information technology; these computer programs perform a rough translation, from English to Spanish for example, and provide a useful first draft for a professional translator. One such program was developed at the Pan American Health Organization (PAHO). It has been used effectively at IRRI and at the CGIAR Secretariat, where staff members have indicated that its vocabulary of life science and chemistry terms has made it very useful. These programs promise to provide a more responsive tool for translators than the services that can be provided by a remote service organization.

Chapter 4

LESSONS LEARNED

Like all communications technologies, e-mail makes demands on organizations and has an impact on their operations. This chapter reviews some of the issues involved in the use of e-mail and some of the lessons learned from experience with CGNET. Issues that concern network users, especially developing-country users, are presented first. Remarks about the network as a whole are presented second.

Choosing the Right Kind of Installation

E-mail, and computer communication in general, are very flexible. Better modems can compensate for noisy telephone lines; telephone lines or computers can be switched when they fail; virtually any computer or word processor can be used to prepare and print messages; and the interaction style can be chosen from a wide variety of options to best fit the organization or person that will use the system.

This very flexibility can make getting on-line a confusing process. There are usually several technological and organizational options from which to choose. A bad choice can sour users' opinions about the service. Several questions should be asked about a location when choosing options.

What sort of communications are available?

Methods of access range from using an inexpensive data network to an expensive data network (in those countries that have data networks); to IDD (where international calls work); to dial-in or satellite service in very difficult regions. The state of local communications services has a large bearing on the style of network interaction that can be supported. On inexpensive data networks, any of the interaction models can be supported. The solitary on-line model (one mailbox for each user) is quite attractive. Where expensive data networks or IDD access is used, the centralized message room model is more cost efficient. The IDD situation requires well-trained operators who can make good use of the time they spend on-line and who know their backup systems well. To reach the network successfully in locations where communication is very difficult, it may be necessary to have someone at the location who knows computers or communications quite well. In all cases, the quality of the local telecommunications services has a very large bearing on the type of modems required for the site.

How available is technical support?

Some locations have a computer centre, complete with staff and mainframe computer resources. Other locations have at least a few full-time technical staff; some rely on local consultants. However, many scientists are posted in towns and cities where no local technicians are available. These researchers must rely on long-distance help, seeking assistance from their centres or e-mail network staff. When a centre or branch office has its own technical staff, more automated solutions, including different types of gateway service, become possible. Local consultants are always available in developed countries and are often available in large cities in developing countries, especially in countries that have local data networks. In these cases, the equipment can be set up, and the training can be conducted entirely with local help. When little or no local support is available, part of the e-mail installation should include a few days of training for the local staff. Usually this training is conducted by a visiting consultant.

How centralized is the organization?

Some centres are administered in a highly centralized way that includes a registry for all communications and restrictions on who can use communication facilities. Other centres are decentralized, and all staff are able to use any communication facilities. Many centres fall between these two extremes, with communications falling under the jurisdiction of a Director of Administration. Although all staff may write messages that will be sent by e-mail, in most cases, only a few people are authorized to log on to the e-mail system and send messages. A message room can be installed in one of the more centralized organizations with little trouble. However, a solitary on-line service can create problems because the system may fail to live up to expectations. Decentralized centres may benefit most from using a number of solitary on-line mailboxes or some kind of gateway system. However, the gateway system may need to include special controls if message authorization is required. If necessary, centres can use the introduction of e-mail to force a change in the communications patterns of the centre, but this will almost certainly slow down acceptance of the system.

What is the communication "profile"?

Some locations have a low volume of message traffic. Others have higher volume with a wide dispersion. Still others have volume with a concentration (most messages go to subcentres or to regional offices). Low-volume locations will probably want to check their mailboxes less often, especially if they have IDD network access. High-volume locations can realize substantial cost savings, especially if they centralize their message handling. Locations that have a concentrated communication profile will benefit most by bringing their subcentres on-line. For these centres, it is often cost effective to plan a coordinated multilocation project; that is, to bring subcentres on-line at the same time as the centre or shortly thereafter.

Starting Off Right

The most critical period is just after the initial installation, when first impressions about the system are formed and when training in system use is conducted. After the type of installation has been chosen, most of the issues are organizational rather than technical.

Dealing with the local telecommunications authorities

Twenty years ago, virtually all nations required permission to connect any communication device to their national telephone systems. Since then, standards for connection have been adopted by many developed countries. In these countries, large classes of devices (including answering machines, wireless telephones, and modems) can now be attached to a telephone line without special permission. However, some developed countries, and most developing countries, still require explicit permission for every telephone device that is installed.

The reasons for this are primarily economic, although security concerns also play a role in decisions to withhold approval. National telephone systems can raise more revenue if users are required to rent or buy telephones from the national telecommunications authority. Modems and facsimile machines can be rented at an especially high premium, and users can be discouraged from getting their own equipment by lengthy national "type-approval" procedures. Another reason for concern on the part of local authorities is that substitution of e-mail or facsimile for telex can lead to a net reduction in their revenue (although this is generally not true of long-run profits because the markup on data communications is higher). Finally, some countries, especially those with a recent history of civil unrest or those in which governments feel their control is insecure, also have military security concerns. Syria, for example, forbids virtually all nongovernment organizations from having modems or other data communications equipment. This has kept ICARDA headquarters off CGNET.

In countries that do not have data networks, it can be hard to find officials who know what modems are and how they work. Yet, there may still be regulations that require registration of modems. Although computer hobbyists in such places often ignore the authorities, international organizations operating under formal agreements with their host governments are normally obligated to follow all regulations. In some cases, however, even the officials instruct the users to ignore the regulations. In India, between 1985 and 1988, users were told that the authorities had no policy; therefore, they should just go ahead, but keep it quiet. In Nigeria in 1987, one user was verbally instructed by an official to ignore the regulations because finding someone with both the knowledge and the authority to issue a permit would be difficult.

In most developing countries, written permission is formally issued, usually by the PTT. It is usually sufficient to specify the type of device that will be used and to indicate that it obeys the relevant international standards. Presenting an analogy with facsimile often helps to speed the approval process. In Nigeria, for example, facsimile permissions were routinely issued in 1989, and they could readily be modified to include permission for a modem and e-mail. If the government requires centres to give a reason for requesting permission to use a modem, it is often helpful to specify that the modem will be used to search remote databases (or "data banks").

Telecommunications authorities are probably most restrictive when they have just begun to operate a data network of their own or are planning to launch one. At these times, they may consider the market too small to support competition from other sources. They usually want to be the exclusive provider of modems and to be sure that all modem owners use their service. Although these modems and services are sometimes adequate, national telecommunications authorities usually do not provide error-correcting modems. Error correction is essential outside the capital city and is a prerequisite for using IDD access as a backup route when the local service fails to operate. When error correction is required and the local data network does not provide it, a special approval may be required to obtain an error-correcting modem. This is usually because the local telecommunications authorities have never seen this type of modem.

Fortunately, most international researchers have sufficient status with their host governments to get such permission — eventually. As with bureaucracies everywhere, telecommunications authorities in most countries are slow, and correct procedures must be followed. In one country, a centre spent 6 months trying to get permission to use the telephone system for data communication. The authorities asked for a description of the application. They then asked for a diagram of the worldwide data network. Finally, they requested a schematic of the modem that would be used! Sensing at this point that something was wrong, the centre administrators paid a visit to the head of operations of the PTT in the capital city. When the project was explained to him, he became quite enthusiastic and immediately granted permission. In many cases where permission was sought and granted, a degree of personal contact was needed to obtain the approval of the PTT. Close contact with the senior staff of the PTT significantly speeded the approval process.

Surprisingly, even in countries that have data networks, it can be time consuming to obtain an account to use the systems. When the service is new, there is often a shortage of information and a surplus of misinformation. In one country, a modem had to be leased from the PTT to get an account. The PTT, however, had no modems and therefore would not issue accounts. People were not allowed to use privately purchased modems. Therefore, an arrangement was worked out that allowed the centre to buy two modems, donate them to the PTT, and then lease them back! Patience and willingness to compromise can often be important when dealing with PTTs in some developing countries.

Fortunately, as national data networks mature, PTTs usually see the potential gains from wider use of their networks, and official policies become more liberal. Most countries eventually stop requiring permission altogether, as have most European and Southeast Asian PTTs. In any case, before dealing with the PTT, it is advisable to identify the correct person in the PTT and to ask advice on procedures from someone who has a modem. Public databases maintained by data networks in the United States and the United

Kingdom contain the names of the PTT contacts, and e-mail providers can sometimes supply names of local users.

Using expert help while setting up

Data communication is not overly difficult; however, everything must be set up properly. There are many variations in equipment configuration, including the internal parameters of the modem, the wires in the cables, and the settings of the interface card and the computer's software. Although most of these are standardized with any one computer platform (such as for IBM-compatible computers and mass-market modems), there are endless variations on other machines and modems.

Variations also exist among the many data networks used to access CGNET from around the world. Some variations are particular to specific countries; other variations are inherent in the use of international telephone calls for data communication. For example, some countries in Africa have much better telephone communications to the United Kingdom (or to France) than to any other country; some have inexpensive off-peak rates to Asian countries. Only by experimentation can the most reliable and least costly routing be found for an e-mail call.

Expert on-site assistance can be particularly useful for institutions that have never used e-mail, or for those that have had limited experience with computers. In some developing country research institutions, no one may have ever logged onto a remote computer system, had previous experience in using communication software, or used the word processing package they will use to prepare their messages. The e-mail computer may even be their first computer. In these cases, it is unreasonable to assume that they will be able to get on-line by themselves. Sending an expert to the site for a week may prevent a year of frustration and costly telexes.

Even organizations that have had experience using telecommunications networks in developed countries can run into problems when they try to bring branch offices in developing countries on-line. Over a period of 3 years, for example, one large organization based in North America tried repeatedly to set up an e-mail network linking its international sites. Despite their previous success with computers and e-mail applications in North America, they did not anticipate the problems they encountered in Africa and India. First, they were unsure of the government arrangements needed to install the e-mail system overseas, which created frustrating delays and setbacks in the approval process. Next, the modems they chose were unsuitable for noisy international telephone lines, which resulted in garbled, unreadable messages. They were also unaware of the easiest and cheapest routes to link into their North American e-mail system from overseas. They decided to call in consultants who were experienced in installing e-mail systems in developing countries. Each branch office was successfully brought on-line and training was completed within 2 weeks.

Although the on-site visits and the new error-correcting modems were costly, these expenditures were recovered through reduced communications costs in less than a year. As this example shows, organizations planning to establish e-mail links in developing countries need to be prepared to deal with some of the problems unique to telecommunications in those countries. The decision of whether or not to use outside specialists must be made considering the resources of the organization, the difficulty of linking a given site to the e-mail network, and the savings expected from having the overseas sites brought on-line quickly. An on-site visit is most likely to pay for itself if the site to be brought on-line is located in a region where communication is still very difficult.

Operator training

The single most important component in successful e-mail installations is training the people who operate the link. The reason for this is inherent to the mailbox structure of e-mail: if you do not check your mailbox, you will not get your mail. Even when message transfers are automated, staff training is still of great importance. Someone will have to fix the system, or at least be able to pick up and send mail manually if anything goes wrong.

Operator training should emphasize the basic ideas behind e-mail and relate these ideas to the commands and responses they need to run their communication software. Operators should also know how to determine when and why something has gone wrong and know how to fix the problem. For example, when the problem is in the telephone line, they should be able to recognize this and switch their modem to a different line. Similarly, when the data network has a problem, they should be able to recognize the symptoms and use a different data network. Finally, if the problem is with the computer, they should know some of the most likely causes and what they might be able to do to fix the problem.

Achieving this level of proficiency is usually possible in 3 to 5 days with a few hours of hands-on training each day. It is a good idea to have the training conducted by an expert, or at least by someone who has successfully trained others before. The operators should be provided with a clearly written handbook that contains instructions for most contingencies. However, it is not enough to simply give new e-mail operators a book and expect them to understand the system. Until operators understand the ideas behind e-mail, their trouble-shooting ability will be limited. The most successful training sessions therefore emphasize hands-on learning and teach people to understand the system rather than to follow a list of instructions. It does take a little more time and effort to provide this kind of training, but the payoff in improved trouble-shooting skills is well worth the additional effort.

Another important consideration is identifying and training the "right people." These people may be junior scientists, programmers, or secretaries; their positions matter less than their desire to learn and their willingness to take responsibility when things go wrong. The quality that seems to make someone the "right person" is having a personal interest in mastering the technology. It is important not to overlook junior staff or support staff when potential e-mail operators are selected. These staff are often even more motivated to learn than senior staff because experience with computers and communications technology is perceived as potentially valuable for career advancement. A number of secretaries in developing country institutions have chosen to work with e-mail as a way of gaining valuable training that they could not have received elsewhere.

Several people should be trained at any one site to ensure that there is always someone on hand who knows how to operate the e-mail system. The best approach is usually to train two people at first and then to set up a rotation with other potential operators for the first month or so. During this period, it is best if trainees work in pairs. They can learn a great deal when working together because no two people pick up exactly the same information from a training session. Ongoing training using e-mail messages has also proven effective for reinforcing procedures learned in the initial training sessions. Remember that operators can only learn so much in a single week; time-saving shortcuts or other information are best communicated after the most important lessons have "sunk in."

Solitary users of CGNET, who use personal computers in cities in a developed country, may be puzzled by this emphasis on training. Many users of this type have gotten on-line themselves, perhaps with a bit of coaching from a nearby computer enthusiast. The difference is that in most organizational settings, a higher level of service is expected because the e-mail operator becomes responsible for the correspondence of other people. Making a mistake with your own messages is tolerated much more easily than making a mistake with a message for someone else. Another important difference is that most CGNET users are located in countries with poor communications systems and that the staff at most centres have had little exposure to computers (and none at all to computer communications). In these cases, the setup is harder, the problems are more numerous, and the nearby sources of help are much less knowledgeable. Given these conditions, the operators must become self-sufficient for the e-mail system to function properly.

Multiple backup alternatives

A central feature of mailbox systems is their reliability and flexibility. The central mailbox computer system operates 24 hours a day and contains several computer systems as a backup. This ensures that the mailbox computer forms the reliable pivot for the network and that numerous alternative routes can be used to access the system. If one access method fails, other routes can be used. For example, if one telephone line has problems, the modem can be connected to another telephone line, with no effect on network service. Similarly, if a local data network is temporarily out of order, users can make an international telephone call and use a different data network to access CGNET.

Learning how to use a backup system can be of key importance in developing-country locations because telephone systems are often unreliable. Network users in these locations should know how to access the network from at least one alternative route, and they may want to consider configuring their communication software to include different access methods. Establishing an alternate route is not difficult, even in developing countries. A number of alternatives exist for accessing the central mailbox system. If a local or regional data network is not working, network members can usually make a long distance call to an international data network. If users customarily call an international data network such as Tymnet, they generally phone a different international network if their regular access number is out of commission.

Using a backup route need not be a difficult process. It is relatively easy to configure communication software packages to include options for many different access routes. In addition, a home telephone and a personal computer can be used as a backup route. In some CGIAR centres, scientists posted in small field offices have chosen this option. On days when the office telephone is not working, they use home computers to access the network.

Backup routes are important even in countries that have data networks. In many developing countries, the local data network consists of a single communication computer that is remote-controlled from the United States, the United Kingdom, France, or another developed country. When the local computer fails for any reason (such as a power failure or an overheated component), it can be shut down for up to a day. In one country, the local network broke down when the e-mail was first installed and did not start up again for another week! When a local breakdown occurs, it is important to have the option of making an international call to pick up or send e-mail messages.

To ensure that operators become conversant with backup procedures, the procedures should be used during the initial training and exercised occasionally to be sure that they still work. Telephone numbers and methods for accessing international data networks change from time to time, and operators can easily forget a procedure or computer command that they do not use often. Occasional use of the backup will ensure that it can be used without problems when it is needed.

Follow the paper flow

Every organization has some way of filing and circulating its correspondence. Most CGIAR centres keep a "chron" file of all external messages in a central place. Some make a copy of all messages and collect them in a "daily file" that is passed to the Director General or circulated among all directors. In most of the IARCs, someone in the Director General's office reviews all incoming messages to determine who should receive copies. Some institutes also require that all outgoing messages be authorized by a senior staff member before they leave the building.

When installing e-mail, it is advisable to examine the flow of correspondence and to decide how the e-mail system can best fit. If the e-mail is incorporated into the existing system, it is more likely to be perceived as a valuable tool; if it operates outside the system, it may be resented. However, the existing policy on correspondence should not always determine the structure of the e-mail system. Some "paper flows" are needlessly complex, and applying the same model to the e-mail system would be inefficient. In these cases, the introduction of an e-mail system can be a good time for administrators to evaluate and possibly simplify existing procedures.

The diffusion process: administrators, then scientists, then others

The first users of a new e-mail system are likely to be the administrators. Many are already accustomed to using electronic media, such as telex and facsimile, and their communications are often costly, sometimes involving thousands of dollars. Administrators who have high communications volumes can be expected to take immediate advantage of any opportunity to speed their work and reduce costs. For example, purchasing officers are often among the first to make use of a new e-mail system. They send many messages each day to request bids, place orders, and trace shipments; therefore, e-mail offers both cost and efficiency advantages. In addition to these advantages, e-mail messages can be typed directly onto a hard disk or floppy diskette and then sent to the e-mail operator to be transmitted. Because messages do not need to be retyped, e-mail cuts down on the errors that can occur when a message must be reinput to be sent as a telex.

Researchers, especially those who already use computers, are usually the next group to make use of a new e-mail system. Younger scientists who have used e-mail systems at their universities usually welcome e-mail as a valuable tool, especially if it allows correspondence with colleagues on the academic networks in other countries. Scientists who have never used e-mail may adopt the system more slowly; however, after they start to use e-mail for their technical correspondence, they begin to see its possibilities.

After an e-mail system becomes well established at a centre, a number of users outside the centre will be brought on-line. For example, one mailbox may be set up for the chairperson to maintain close contact with the director; another might be set up to help scientists on tour or on leave keep in touch with colleagues or assistants conducting experiments. Regional offices and programs are frequently brought on-line next to ease communication between the branch offices and the administrators at headquarters. This sort of growth typically begins 3 to 6 months after a centre has come on-line.

How It Catches On: Two Scenarios

Usage of a new e-mail system can vary a great deal depending on the attitudes of the people in the organization. Two scenarios are used to illustrate the more common experiences.

Scenario 1. High-level backing

The amount of work required to bring an international centre on-line is considerable; without a champion at the centre of the organization, the task is nearly impossible. Moreover, getting on-line requires input and cooperation on the part of many different divisions of an organization. The various tasks that must be undertaken when preparing to adopt an e-mail system cut across organizational responsibilities. For example, obtaining the necessary communications equipment implies a capital equipment purchase — something that may require input from the budget committee, as well as the administration and purchasing divisions. The next step, setting up electronic mailbox accounts, involves a contractual agreement. Again, a number of different departments may be involved, ranging from the administration and communications divisions to the government liaison office. Similarly, allocating a telephone line for the network or installing a special line that bypasses the switchboard may require the services of in-house technical staff, as well as assistance from local electricians or telephone technicians. Next, someone in the government liaison office may have to approach the PTT to obtain a data network account, or to get permission to operate a modem. Manuals and documentation must be ordered and placed in an accessible location. Finally, someone has to learn how to use the system and train e-mail operators. Each one of these steps may require approval from a number of different divisions, and some may require the approval of government authorities as well.

When many different divisions are involved, explicit support from the Director of administration and finance or the Director General is essential to get a large organization on-line. Only someone who has the authority to speak for the entire centre can easily coordinate all the resources needed to bring the centre on-line successfully. Therefore, it is often worth working first to secure the support of administration by emphasizing the potential of e-mail to reduce costs and increase productivity.

In CGIAR centres where support from administrators was highly visible, the process of adopting an e-mail system moved smoothly and quickly; in centres without the benefit of clear administrative backing, attempts to get on-line stalled and frequently failed. In a number of cases, a library, an information services department, a computer centre, or a scientific program wanted to use CGNET, but they were unable to muster the necessary resources to take care of all the details themselves. The amount of time required to take care of the prerequisites was the first barrier they encountered in trying to get on-line. Because the rest of the organization did not perceive a need for e-mail, the staff in these departments found themselves responsible for all the tasks involved in the process. They all had other work to do and were unable to devote the amount of time needed to get on-line. A second barrier that discouraged individual departments from pursuing their interest in e-mail was the fear that they would be penalized for engaging in an activity beyond the scope of their operation. In contrast, in centres where the e-mail system had the support of the Director General or administration, no one division was burdened with all the tasks involved in getting the centre on-line, and no division feared being penalized for devoting time to the cause.

Explicit endorsement from a Director General or an Assistant Director General both speeds the installation process and ensures that the new e-mail system will be well used. When a centre policy is established that favours e-mail usage, obstacles can disappear overnight and usage can rise rapidly. In one organization where network usage had remained low since the system was adopted, support from the Director General was all it took to increase the usage of the network. At a meeting of senior staff at the centre, the Director General announced: "Folks we're here to grow more crops and feed more people. What Georg [Lindsey] is saying makes sense to me, and I don't understand why we're not doing it. I want to see us make use of this system, or I want some explanation." The usage of the network during the previous year was minor compared with the usage in the next few months.

Scenario 2. The lonely innovator and the conversion experience

In some centres, efforts to install CGNET were focused more than had been foreseen on "motivating" the staff to take an interest in, and to take advantage of, the new system. Certainly it was true that once centre staff were convinced of the options and the benefits CGNET provided, they wanted to take advantage of them. But the initial convincing required a great deal of time. In this scenario, efforts to establish e-mail were initially met with skeptical statements such as: "It's been tried before, and it doesn't work here."

The effort to get on-line typically began with an interested individual who had enough technical expertise (or blind perseverance) to follow through on all the necessary preliminaries. This meant, among other things, obtaining a licence, procuring a modem and successfully hooking it up to the computer, and mastering the communication software. This "setup" stage often required several calendar months and was frequently stressful for the "innovator." On top of their regular job responsibilities, these innovators were responsible for the seemingly endless tasks involved in establishing a connection to CGNET.

Once the setup was complete, learning to use CGNET was not overly difficult. Unfortunately, by this time, the innovators sometimes faced a motivation problem or had little time to devote to familiarizing themselves with the network. Despite their original intention to "spread the word," some of the initial enthusiasm had worn off when they finally got on-line. At that point, the innovator was also likely to be behind in his or her "regular" work. A lull in usage of the newly acquired e-mail capability followed.

In most centres where the e-mail system was first championed by a single innovator, usage of CGNET only became widespread after the network proved instrumental in conveying an urgent message or report to a far away sponsor, a travelling staff member, or a collaborating researcher. News of the success followed rapidly and, soon, the innovator (now hero) was besieged with requests to use the "new" service. Requests were sent daily for general information about computers and communication and for instructions on how to use the e-mail facilities. Administrators who were previously apathetic or even antagonistic became converts. At that point, the CGNET facility was considered "installed," and the service was usually reorganized to serve the whole institute without overloading the original innovator.

Organizational reasons for delay

Occasionally, even high-level support may not be sufficient to ensure speedy implementation of a CBMS. For example, someone who is given the task of operating the CBMS may already feel overworked and may resist the new responsibility. Occasionally, one department may feel threatened by allowing another department to handle messages or to influence its operations. And sometimes, remote scientists, or even a centre, may prefer the isolation they currently enjoy and may not want closer links with administration or other entities.

In situations like these, a visit by an expert can be particularly helpful. An outside expert can resolve technical issues, answer questions from centre staff, and dispel misconceptions about the e-mail system. In addition, the presence of a consultant on a short visit can add a kind of deadline pressure that eliminates foot-dragging. If the consultant has high-level backing, foot-dragging and other problems will be quickly resolved.

One extreme example illustrates the point. One centre was initially unable to get on-line because they had no computer for the CBMS. To overcome this barrier, they were given a computer, a modem, and some communication software. Several months later, another problem surfaced: how could they get in touch with the PTT? Contact information was found and provided. Then, the software did not work. It turned out that the software was working, but that no one had learned how to use it. Then, the user manuals were misplaced. After 18 months of problem after problem, an on-site visit was arranged. When the consultant arrived at the site, it took about 2 hours to get all of the details resolved and to get the e-mail system completely operational. In this case, the deadline pressure established by the short length of the visit eliminated the foot-dragging that had delayed implementation of the e-mail system.

Fortunately, very few centres seem to suffer from these problems for long. With a little assistance, a site can quickly be set up, and organizational issues can be worked out.

Accelerators of progress

When an organization decides to use e-mail, a number of steps can be taken to accelerate progress. Conducting a presentation, a series of demonstrations, or a workshop can rapidly familiarize everyone with the service. These activities can also address worries that work routines or "turf boundaries" will be disrupted.

E-mail offers great potential for eliminating tedious work. Unlike telexes, e-mail messages can be saved onto diskettes or submitted using a central mainframe computer. They do not need to be reinput, so errors are less likely. In addition, telexes, facsimiles, and short e-mail messages can all be copied onto one disk and sent out over the network. These simplifications and improvements in the work flow can be powerful motivators for using the system, because no one likes dull, repetitive work such as reinputting and proofreading messages. Secretaries, who are responsible for handling most message traffic at the centres, are usually eager to adopt any tool that improves their efficiency. Steps that rationalize and improve the message flow in the centre will accelerate the adoption of the CBMS, but only if people know about them. Pointing out the advantages of using the e-mail system will, therefore, help to speed acceptance and usage of the system.

Another incentive that hastens acceptance of e-mail is to set up a grace period in which departments or staff members can use the system without being charged. Most centres did this to encourage staff to use the system. Because e-mail was so much less expensive than telex, there was little advantage to internal billing at first. However, after usage built up and stabilized, the centres generally began to charge individual departments for their use. Even then, however, simple estimates of costs often sufficed for internal billing purposes.

Regulating the Pace of Change

The technology of data communications changes rapidly. New access methods, modems, software, and services are introduced every year. In Africa alone, new IDD access methods have become available every year for the last 3 years, and new national data networks are constantly being set up. The same is true in other regions. Changes are just as rapid in the hardware and software fields. Given this situation, users can easily be overwhelmed by trying to keep up with the latest technology. The questions become: how long should they keep their equipment and when should they consider replacement? In economic terms, it makes the most sense to keep working equipment for at least 2 years, rather than changing every 6 months just for the sake of keeping up.

Similarly, there are limits to how much information individuals can absorb about new technology. New network users are advised to take the first few weeks or months slowly to avoid becoming overwhelmed. Users should begin by focusing on basic message transfer. As they become familiar with the network, they will see its potential for other uses, such as transfers of documents or binary files containing experimental data, and will be prepared to attempt those new applications. At that time, they will be able to anticipate problems and know the proper questions to ask. Before then, too many new ideas can confuse users about how the system works and what it can and cannot do.

Organizations can only absorb so much change at once. It is best if e-mail providers maintain a gradual pace of change so that each new procedure can "sink in" before the next step is attempted. New applications of the CBMS, upgrades to equipment and software used for e-mail, and changes in the personnel who operate the e-mail system, should all be introduced slowly. To help ensure a gradual pace of change, CGNET Services introduces new techniques and applications in a staggered fashion. These services are offered initially to users who seem ready to make good use of them and later to those who are not as familiar with the system.

Supporting the Whole Network

In many ways, CGNET has followed a path similar to that followed by multinational companies and industries such as airlines. Modern communications technology has been used to serve a set of users with similar needs and a common purpose. Many multinational companies have established a "profit centre" or a "consortium," whose mission is to operate and promote a special-purpose network for its members. These independent network centres normally support themselves by charging fees for their services. Consequently, the consortium that operates the network has an incentive to seek out and adapt new technologies for the group, but it is also constrained to do what is economically worthwhile. Fee-for-service networks are kept on track by their users because they must remain sensitive to user needs and offer only those services for which users are willing to pay.

For the international agricultural research centres, CGNET Services International has acted as this self-financing network support group. In addition to administering the network and recovering its costs, CGNET Services provides technical advice and consulting for small-scale users and serves as an additional resource for the technical staff at larger research centres.

Although the overall reaction to having an independent network support group has been positive, some limitations are imposed by its independence. One limitation is the inability to guarantee uniformity in service standards or benefits across different institutions. Because users participate voluntarily and are not bound by a commitment to use the network, service standards may differ between otherwise similar institutions. One organization may check its mail several times a day and put all its telecommunications through the network; whereas, another organization in the same city may hardly use the system. This can be inconvenient for users who send mail through the network and expect a quick response. It can also prove costly; potential savings are lost when telex or facsimile are used instead of e-mail.

In addition, users of an independent network cannot be required to make a change, even if it would improve the service of the network as a whole. In a few CGNET locations, obsolete or faulty equipment was not replaced for months after problems surfaced, which resulted in unreliable service and wasted money. Similarly, organizational problems may persist until they become acute. Again the result may be decreased efficiency and wasted resources. Network support personnel may have suggestions for resolving both technical and organizational problems, but they must be careful when approaching personnel at these centres. Trying to get users to make a change can be counterproductive in some cases; centre computer staff may decide to "go it alone" if they perceive the recommendations made by network consultants as an intrusion on their areas of responsibility. Although an independent support group may know the solution to a problem, it lacks the authority to put it in place.

Problems like these have been rather rare in CGNET. First, a good network connection saves money, and this by itself has been an incentive to upgrade obsolete equipment. In addition, a number of centres consider their CGNET connection an example of their technical competence and value it as a kind of status symbol. This factor also keeps centres interested in suggested improvements.

Coordinated projects must be approached a bit differently by an outside support group. If several potential users are located in a single geographic area, the most economical and effective approach would be to get them all on-line in one visit. However, because each organization has separate budgetary constraints and a different decision-making process, it may not be possible to organize a coordinated e-mail implementation project. Similarly, cost sharing with regard to field tests of new technology (such as a new type of modem) can be difficult. Even if the new technology promises to become widely used after successful field trials, it can be nearly impossible to get all the likely users to agree to share the costs of the trial. Cost-sharing and coordination problems like these have slowed the adoption of new technology, but have not been insurmountable. Usually, one user wants the visit or trial badly enough to underwrite the entire cost; if other users join in, costs can be somewhat reduced. Alternatively, the network support group can fund the initial effort and eventually divide the costs among users when they adopt the new application or technology.

Communicating with Other Message Systems

Connecting to academic networks

In developed countries, most university computer centres are linked to some sort of network. These academic networks have names like BITNET in the United States, NetNorth in Canada, EARN in most of Europe, JANET in Britain, and JUNET in Japan. The large Internet network links the mainframe computers of universities, major research institutes, and some private companies and allows their users to exchange messages and data files. In addition, Internet has gateways to each of the other academic networks. Because these networks reach very large populations of scholars, it is essential for research-oriented institutions to establish electronic connections to the academic networks.

A gateway service permits CGNET users to exchange messages and most types of data files with academic network users. Sending messages through the gateway is not quite as simple as it would be with a direct connection to Internet, nor is it as fast because the gateway can impose delays of a few hours in message transmission. Despite its limitations, however, the Internet–CGNET gateway is widely used by diverse groups. To give just a few examples: a maize breeder in Zimbabwe maintains regular contact with his former thesis advisor; a software specialist in the Philippines subscribes to a European bulletin board on computer viruses; and animal disease researchers in Kenya exchange bacterial DNA sequences with colleagues at a university in Florida.

Direct connection between mainframe computers in developing country centres and the academic networks has been tried and continues to be studied. This type of direct connection would be faster and would permit a user's mainframe computer to act as an "information server" that would automatically process requests for data from users of the academic networks. So far, however, the costs appear to be high and the additional benefits are rather low.

A direct connection requires a full-time data link between the user's mainframe computer and a computer on the academic network. These links are not expensive within a developed country, especially when nearby computers are already on the network. However, for an isolated centre in a developing country, the link would be very expensive (typically thousands of dollars per month) because it would be an international or even intercontinental link. In addition, new computer equipment would have to be purchased, and additional management responsibilities would fall on centre computer staff. This could be a significant burden because the academic networks have little central network support. Computer centre staff might find themselves responsible for maintaining directories, working out message routing or addressing problems, and debugging telecommunications problems, in addition to their regular work.

The benefits of the link would include somewhat greater simplicity for users at the centre and the ability to effectively "publish" databases for users of the academic networks. These are rather small gains because the most important clients of the international agricultural research centres are in the developing countries, and these clients do not have network links themselves.

A more cost-effective mainframe connection has been put in place in a few centres. These central computers are linked as host computers on the public data network in their country using the "X.25" protocol. This link is much less expensive because it does not require a full-time international data circuit; billing is based on the amount of usage (rather than per day or per month). Because benefits and costs rise together, it is easier to manage. In addition, these network links can be used to carry ordinary CGNET messages and make database inquiries on computers all over the world.

New types of academic network connections have been developed that allow X.25 links to carry academic network traffic (these connections have already been used in Europe). However, most of the academic networks now use and will continue to use non-X.25

protocols. To bridge the gap between the X.25 network and the academic network, the original CGNET was extended using a new computer that is on both networks. This CGNET II computer permits centres to draw from databases, file archives, and other services on the academic networks and to contribute data to a file archive maintained on the bridge machine. For mail processing, CGNET II provides an improved message gateway with simpler message addressing, faster message delivery, and a centralized directory.

As communications technology advances, new types of networking evolve. Universities in developed countries are often at the cutting edge. Researchers in developing countries have fewer choices. To serve the researchers on CGNET, "internetworking" has become increasingly important.

Connecting with facsimile

When CGNET was originally formed, facsimile machines had been invented, but were too expensive for ordinary use. Subsequently, the price of the machines fell dramatically and a "critical mass" of facsimile owners was formed. Since 1988, sending messages by "fax" has become commonplace. In many organizations, especially in developed countries, facsimile has become the preferred message transfer technology.

Like the academic networks, the "network" of facsimile machines contains many correspondents with whom IARCs communicate regularly. Facsimile technology has many special attributes that make it complementary to the role played by e-mail. A number of factors must be considered when evaluating the proper use of facsimile in any institution: the cost of telephone calls; the quality of telephone connections; and the time spent by personnel to send facsimiles.

Early facsimile machines (group one and group two machines) were analog and very slow. The "group three" facsimile machines, which were much faster than their predecessors, became popular in the 1980s. Just as with e-mail, "group three" machines use digital modems and telephone lines to achieve message transfer at lower cost than telex. Facsimile machines are also completely standardized, which makes installation relatively simple. A facsimile machine resembles a photocopy machine and is almost as easy to use. It can transmit anything that can be put on paper, including drawings and any written alphabet. Facsimile is a good choice when telephone lines are of good quality, when the volume of messages to be sent is fairly low, and when centres must transmit documents that have not already been input into a computer.

For communication within a metropolitan area, facsimile can be nearly perfect. The quality of the telephone call is usually good and the cost of each facsimile call is low. A number of CGIAR centres, including IRRI and WARDA, keep one facsimile machine at headquarters and another at their capital city liaison offices. They use their facsimile machines to transmit documents such as customs declarations and airbills instantly, thus eliminating a major source of delay.

For international organizations in developing countries, however, there can be other problems. Telephone lines cannot always be used by a facsimile machine and telephone service may be of very poor quality. A facsimile machine works best when a telephone line is dedicated for facsimiles. This allows incoming messages to be taken automatically by the machine and means that the telephone line is not constantly busy. Because it can be difficult to get additional telephone lines in many developing countries, an existing telephone line may have to be split between the facsimile machine and regular telephone use by one of the departments at the centre. In this case, centre personnel must be notified with a telephone call that someone would like to send a document by facsimile. Much of the convenience associated with facsimile technology is lost if a correspondent must first call to ensure that the line is switched over to the facsimile machine.

Another problem in developing countries is that telephone lines fail frequently. When the facsimile line is out of service, outgoing messages can be sent by moving the facsimile machine to a different line, but incoming messages cannot be received unless correspondents are notified of the new telephone number. CBMS, in contrast, allows users to both send and receive messages from any telephone line. They can call out from any working telephone line and can both send and receive messages during any given call.

International facsimile calls also present more of a problem than calls within metropolitan areas. Some international telephone lines simply will not carry a facsimile signal. In mid-1989, for example, CIP (near Lima, Peru) could not send facsimile messages to its offices in Beijing, Cameroon, or Tunisia. Similarly, many locations have trouble sending facsimiles to Nigeria or India. From the United States, it can still take three or four tries to send a facsimile successfully to Africa. CBMS overcomes this difficulty because users call out to a local or regional access point to send and receive all messages, and they can choose that access point that is most reliable for them.

Another difficulty is presented by noisy telephone lines. Noise can cause whole lines of a message to be lost or distorted. The recipient must then ask the sender to try again, a process that can add a delay of a day when there is a large time difference between the two locations. To reduce errors on noisy lines, facsimile machines frequently slow down, which can double or quadruple transmission time and does not totally eliminate errors. CBMS connections, in contrast, can use error-correcting modems to eliminate all traces of noise. CBMS mailboxes also hold a message for several days. Even if a user does not have access to error correction, this feature still allows messages to be picked up another time, when line quality is less of a problem.

Facsimile calls also tend to be longer than CBMS calls and are, therefore, more expensive. From developing countries, an average page takes 40 to 50 seconds to send by facsimile; the same page can be sent by CBMS in 10 or 20 seconds. CBMS also tends to be cheaper because a number of messages can be sent with each individual call. This becomes especially important when calls are billed in 3-minute or even 1-minute increments. Finally, a major advantage of shorter CBMS calls is that they are less likely to be disconnected, so the number of redials is minimized.

In organizations that send many messages, a facsimile machine can be a bottleneck. Lines of people waiting to use the facsimile machine build up at some centres, especially during busy times of the year. In addition, when the facsimile is busy sending, it cannot receive messages. Therefore, correspondents must wait until the line is clear before they can send messages outside the centre. CBMS, in contrast, can be used by many people at the same time, both for sending and receiving messages.

Facsimile messages are subject to other problems as well. All group one and group two machines, and most models in use today, print incoming messages on special light-weight paper that is easily damaged and more difficult to file than regular paper. Most facsimile paper loses its image with time and exposure to light; a message can be completely erased after 12 months of sitting in a file drawer. More important, facsimile messages arrive on paper; whereas, CBMS messages arrive in "machine-readable" text and can be forwarded to others without the loss in quality that is a common problem when photocopies are made of a facsimile. Messages received on the e-mail system can be stored in a computer and are easily retrieved when needed. They can also be passed on to other correspondents or brought into a word processing program for revision.

For reasons of cost and convenience, many CGNET users send almost all their facsimile messages through the network (the facsimile "refiling" service described in Chapter 3). For one organization in Beijing, refiling of facsimile communications cut their telephone bills in half. The same is true for CGNET users in Côte d'Ivoire. At the same time, use of the network eliminated garbled messages and the delays caused by lengthy facsimile calls and attempts to retransmit documents. Refiling is not a complete solution, however. First, Dialcom facsimiles do not yet include letterhead or signature, nor do they allow drawings or other graphics to be transmitted. Second, refiling is a better option for international facsimile messages than for local facsimile transmissions. Local or regional facsimiles can usually be sent more economically using a facsimile machine than by using CGNET. Third, a facsimile machine is still needed to receive communications from institutions that prefer to use facsimile and to send drawings or other papers to correspondents.

However, for general international communications, e-mail remains the method of choice because of the ease of access, the speed of transmission, the lower cost, the ability to reach many correspondents with a single call, and the ability to maintain information in a computer-readable form. In fact, many centres that own facsimile machines prefer to send their facsimile messages by CGNET because they save the time they would have spent printing their messages and waiting for a facsimile connection, and they can also send copies to others on the e-mail system with one telephone call. As computerization of research institutes increases, CBMS can be expected to play an expanding role in communication among international research centres.

Chapter 5

THE FUTURE OF CGNET

CGNET is a mature system that has its own momentum for continued improvement. Centres have come to rely on the network and are willing to upgrade equipment regularly. New modems and software are purchased when appropriate and new programs and procedures are continually developed to make the system easier to use. The network continues to expand because additional IARCs join to become better connected to their peers. Some donor organizations have linked CGNET to their internal communication networks.

Many opportunities for growth remain. This chapter reviews options that would allow expansion and improvement of the network. It also describes other information technologies that would complement existing network services.

More Users

CBMS technology has spread rapidly throughout the international agricultural research community. Users on CGNET can exchange messages with counterparts in universities, in many United Nations institutions, and in many donor organizations. A critical mass has been established that increases the value of a connection with each additional user of CGNET.

This phenomenon, of each new network user increasing the value of the network to all other users, is a synergism fundamental to telecommunication networks. As the network grows, it becomes more likely that a correspondent can be reached by e-mail rather than by telex, facsimile, or mail. It also becomes more likely that everyone on an organization's distribution list has a mailbox on the e-mail system. A network connection therefore becomes much more valuable for the next new user.

Some agricultural research organizations do remain outside the network. Many could benefit from having a direct CGNET connection or a gateway between CGNET and their internal e-mail systems. These organizations include

➤ Donor organizations that fund agricultural research;

➤ Scientific organizations in related disciplines, such as resource management, forestry, and environmental studies;

➤ Scientists posted away from their headquarters (at research sites or in national institutes); and

➤ National research institutions in developing countries.

A number of donor organizations (such as ACIAR, Ford Foundation, IDRC, IFAD, Rockefeller Foundation, USAID, Winrock International, and the World Bank) use CGNET to communicate with the organizations whose research they fund. Other donors that fund agricultural research are likely to establish links to the network once they learn about its cost savings and convenience, both for them and for their recipient organizations. CGNET can be used for both internal and external communications if the donors do not already have internal systems. Alternatively, donor organizations that have internal networks can establish gateways to link their internal networks with CGNET, just as IDRC, the Ford Foundation, and the World Bank have done.

A number of resource management research institutes and CGIAR affiliates are already on the network. This group includes AVRDC, IBSRAM, ICLARM, ICRAF, and IIMI, as well as some of their branch offices. These institutes communicate frequently with agricultural research institutes because both types of research institutes view ecological and resource issues as basic aspects of sustainable agriculture. As more and more institutes recognize the interrelationship of these concerns, researchers at resource management organizations can be expected to communicate increasingly with agriculturalists.

Centre representatives at field offices are a special case because they have a low volume of communications and often work in locations where communication is difficult. When they are in cities that have data network nodes, e-mail works very well for them because the system can be accessed, either from home or office, at low cost. In locations where international telephone calls are required, high telephone bills can negate most of the cost savings that e-mail normally offers low-volume users. However, cost savings are not always the primary concern. Despite the high cost of using IDD access, many institutes consider it important to keep all their outposts on the network because it keeps them equally in touch. As technologies progress and communications infrastructures improve, the technological and financial barriers to usage can be expected to disappear. Eventually, nearly all branch offices and other institute representatives can be expected to use the network.

National research institutes are potentially a very important user group. The mission of the CGIAR system includes building a close relationship with national researchers and helping them strengthen their research and extension programs. In recent years, sharing of research results between the centres and national researchers, and coordinating research work among all types of researchers, have become high priorities for the CGIAR system. The national systems have only just begun to use CGNET, mainly because most have less computer experience and lower communications budgets than the international agricultural research centres. Like the field office representatives or independent consultants, they tend to be low-volume users with many of the same access problems.

Many national research systems are aware of CGNET — inquiries have been received from places as varied as the University of Botswana, the African Academy of Science, and the Pakistan Agricultural Research Council — but few national research systems have taken the initiative to get on-line. In some cases, the impetus for getting on-line was provided by research teams from cooperative development projects. This is especially likely if the collaborating organization is already on the network. For example, an IITA/USAID project in Cameroon came on-line in 1990. A researcher at Centro para la Investigación en Sistemas Sostenibles Agropecuarios (CIPAV) in Colombia, who works closely with CIAT, came on-line in 1991, and researchers at the Malaysian Agricultural Research and Development Institute (MARDI), who conduct cooperative research with IRRI, joined the network early in 1991. Early in 1992, CIP's collaborator at PROINPA (Promotora Industrial Panamericana) in Bolivia joined CGNET, followed by the Rural Development Administration (RDA) in the Republic of Korea, and an Uruguayan collaborator of the International Fertilizer Development Center (IFDC). These network installations should help to demonstrate the value of a network connection to the national institutes and should encourage them to stay on-line after their cooperative projects have been completed.

Progress in Telecommunications

Telecommunications technology and infrastructure are changing rapidly. Each change makes e-mail easier, cheaper, or more broadly available — sometimes all at the same time. This section examines the likely impact of these changes on the future of CGNET.

Improved data networks

In all industrialized countries and many developing countries, computer networks can be reached with a local or "in-country" telephone call to a node of one of the international telecommunication providers. The scope and reliability of the global data network is expanding rapidly, while the cost is dropping. In the last 5 years, most countries in Latin America and Southeast Asia have established data network access. In 1987, Egypt established its own data network, and, in 1989, India, Senegal, and Cameroon began data networks. Several other countries followed from 1990 to 1992 (Kenya, Sri Lanka, and Niger). In countries that have offered data services for several years, many have cut their rates. For example, some network providers in the Philippines halved their rates during 1987 and 1988. Meanwhile, the existing data networks are gradually being upgraded. Reliability has been improved and new cities are receiving service from local nodes. In Indonesia, for example, it is now possible to call into the data network from 10 regional centres; a comparable number of local nodes are operational in countries such as Brazil, India, Mexico, and the Philippines.

Networks in 40 countries now have facilities that allow communication costs to be billed directly to a user's CGNET account, which bypasses the need to establish individual accounts with the national agency. This arrangement has benefitted travellers and new users, and has greatly increased the number of backup connection routes. Charging communication costs directly to a CGNET account is ideal for travellers, who usually do not have individual accounts with data networks in all of the countries they visit. It is also much simpler for new CGNET users because it allows them to get on-line without first arranging a local account. Arrangements with these networks are also useful for users that need a backup facility. Not only are increased numbers of backup routes available, they can now be accessed with greater ease.

Better modems and data compression

In the past, noisy connections made data transmission problematic from many developing countries, especially when IDD access was used to connect to the network. In recent years, error-correcting modems have been introduced on many data networks. Modems with error correction send data back and forth across the line until it is received without distortion; this eliminates the "garbage" data produced by noise on the telephone line. This technology has made it possible to use even very bad connections for data transmission. Error-correcting modems have been instrumental in making CGNET accessible from many more locations, especially in Africa and South Asia.

When an expensive international call is used to reach CGNET, the speed of the modem is the most important factor in determining the cost of the CGNET connection. Modem speed is measured in characters per second. Faster modems can send or receive more letters or digits during each second of a telephone call. In the last 5 years,

modem speed has tripled, significantly decreasing the cost of accessing the network. In 1985, typical speeds for commercial modems
were 30 to 120 characters per second. By 1988, 120 to 240 characters
per second were typical. By 1992, modems that could process 960
characters per second were commonplace. Within 1 or 2 years, these
modems can be expected to be available on many data networks and
to further speed access to CGNET.

Data compression is another important technology that has
decreased the cost of using the network. The amount of time it takes
to send a character, and therefore the cost of transmission, can be
reduced by detecting regularities in the way letters are used. For
example, in English, "e" is more frequently used than "z" and "t" is
more likely to be followed by "h" than by "p." Data compression
exploits these regularities, doubling or even quadrupling the speed
of data transmission. Compression can be handled by some types of
modems, and, in some systems, it is handled by the computers on
both ends of the connection. Among CGNET users, data compression
was initially used in 1989, primarily for links with Africa and South
Asia. It is now more widely used for transmitting data, as it offers
cost savings to all users.

Combining faster modems and data compression will give rise
to dramatically faster transmission speeds. Today, the average
CGNET user transfers messages to and from the system at about 170
characters per second; new technologies can increase that to over
2 000 characters per second. Organizations, even in remote locations, may in future transfer substantial batches of messages and
data over telephone lines in "blips" of 1 minute or less. Transmitting
data in this way will dramatically lower operating costs and encourage use of the network for sending long documents. In addition,
faster modems and data compression may allow substantial use of
the network to become a reality for national agricultural research
services that currently are constrained by the high cost of IDD access.

Direct satellite links

Nearly all research centres, and most representative scientists, have
telephone lines capable of making international calls. But some

representatives and many research stations have no telephone at all, or have a telephone that cannot reliably complete international calls. Making international calls to check a mailbox can be very costly. In some locations, the cost of checking for mail, whether it is picked up or not, can amount to as much as 50 USD per day. If only a few messages are sent each day, this operating cost can be too high.

For these difficult locations, a satellite connection may be the best option. Using compact and even portable equipment, any place in the world can now communicate directly with a satellite. The equipment typically costs between 5 000 and 15 000 USD to install, and usage charges depend on which satellite system is employed. The most promising and most widely available system, run by the International Maritime Satellite Consortium (Inmarsat), charges strictly by how much it is used; another, based on VSAT (very small aperture terminal) technology and the satellites run by the International Satellite Consortium (Intelsat), charges a flat monthly fee.

The technology and the economics of both systems are appealing, especially when centres are faced with telephone links that do not work. The biggest hurdles to using these systems are the regulations that control their use. Most developing countries prohibit the installation of satellite transmission equipment unless special permission is obtained from the telecommunications authorities or from the government itself. As is the case with the regulation of modems (see Chapter 4), both economic and national security interests may lead a government to restrict private communications options. Satellite equipment is especially likely to be prohibited in countries that have military security problems; these countries find satellite communication worrisome because it completely bypasses the conventional telecommunications system. Even in countries where permission is routinely granted, the telecommunications authority often exacts a high price. For example, as of early 1989, installation of a VSAT device involved a 20 000 USD one-time fee in Sri Lanka and, in Nigeria, a license to install an Inmarsat device cost 10 000 USD.

Despite these hurdles, satellite systems have great promise for extending network usage to places where access is impossible.

Inmarsat is now marketing a message-oriented satellite system for use in developing countries (the Standard-C system). Recognizing the importance of government restrictions, the Inmarsat organization has also pursued negotiations with many developing countries and has thereby lessened regulatory barriers to using satellite equipment.

Regulatory barriers have recently decreased in Nigeria and several other African countries. In late 1991, IITA took advantage of a liberalized regulatory environment in Nigeria to install an Inmarsat satellite dish. Although previous attempts to obtain permission for a satellite had been drawn out for years, liberalization allowed IITA to obtain the necessary approval and install their satellite dish within 6 months.

Another encouraging development occurred at the 1992 World Administrative Radio Conference (WARC). Negotiations at the 1992 WARC resulted in the allocation of several frequencies to global satellite-based messaging. In addition, many developing countries agreed to this new regime, primarily in the expectation of obtaining advantageous profit-sharing arrangements.

Packet radio links

In locations where satellite access is restricted or expensive, packet radio offers a possible solution. Many centres have research sites that are linked to the centre by radio. Although these radio links are sometimes problematic for communications, they do provide basic voice contact. In addition, government authorities have been more willing to licence radio links than satellite links because they are normally only used for domestic communication and can be more easily jammed if required by security situations.

The same radios used for voice communication can also be used to transmit messages and other computer data. Just as computers can communicate using modems over a telephone line, they can also communicate using "packet radio modems" (called terminal node controllers or TNCs) and a radio link. Packet radio was developed by amateur radio enthusiasts during the 1970s and 1980s, but it has just recently become a commercial technology.

The difficulty with packet radio is that it cannot be used for a direct international connection to conventional networks. It must be used to connect to a relay computer, normally in the same country as the user. Consider an experimental station that has a radio link with a research centre. If both the station and the centre have computers with packet radio modems, messages can be exchanged. But for those messages to reach CGNET users, the centre must relay them. For large centres with computer centres and technical staff, this is not a big problem. However, if the centre does not have these resources, it may be impossible to maintain a reliable link between the experimental station and CGNET.

Because of these limitations, packet radio is likely to be adopted by only a few centres and then only to communicate with their in-country research stations. In the future, packet radio technology might gain in importance if developing countries install their own national packet radio systems with links to international networks. This has already been proposed in India and Eritrea.

Inbound IDD service

In some cases, access to CGNET could only be reliably established with telephone calls initiated by CGNET Services. For example, inbound IDD service was provided for ICRISAT from 1985 to 1989. CGNET's computers called ICRISAT's computers in Hyderabad, India, twice each day to transfer messages and data. Initially, this service was established because international calls could not be completed using the telephones in Hyderabad.

From time to time, CSI has conducted other inbound IDD services on an ad hoc basis. The service has also been considered as a standard package. Telephone calls from the United States to most developing countries are much less expensive than calls made in the opposite direction (typically half the price). Inbound IDD service can therefore be used to keep costs down for low-volume users or for users in locations with expensive or difficult telephone service.

So far, however, there has not been much demand for this service. Users consistently prefer to maintain as much control as possible over their use of the network. They want to set the frequencies and exact times of the e-mail calls for themselves and to change them whenever they wish. This minimizes possible difficulties of coordination when conditions change (for example, when telephone lines are out of order, when a user changes location, or when a solitary user goes on leave). Inbound IDD services are not likely to grow, except perhaps in centres that adopt automated gateways.

Progress in Services and Software

In addition to changes in telecommunications hardware, new software and services can also be expected to affect the future of CGNET. New software installed in the CGNET mailbox computers and in the users' computers will significantly enhance the quality of the e-mail service.

Gateways for desk-to-desk correspondence

Since it was first developed in the 1970s, the vision that has motivated CBMS technology has been the desire to create paperless, "desk-to-desk" communication. For much of the CGNET community, that vision has already been realized. Those who use individual mailboxes and those who have connected internal systems directly to CGNET are already sending their messages and data around the world directly from their desktop PCs. For others communicating over CGNET, messages pass through an e-mail operator in a message room. These users generally pass messages along on floppy disks. This situation is changing rapidly. In the near future, most centres are likely to employ an automated gateway to move their messages. The reasons for this shift are that automation

➤ Provides more predictable and efficient service;

➤ Simplifies the learning process for new users;

➤ Increases the integration and uniformity of intracampus, CGNET, telex, and facsimile communications; and

➤ Increases immediacy and confidentiality because users can send their own messages without the involvement of others.

In the past, gateways were difficult to arrange for the centres because most professionals did not have their own computer terminals. Today, however, professionals at most IARCs use PCs. Just as at most companies and universities around the world, IARC staff are increasingly being tied together into local data communications networks. Some centres, including CIMMYT, IRRI, ICRISAT, ISNAR, and CIP are connecting the PCs to a central mainframe computer; others, such as IBPGR, ICRAF, IFPRI, ILCA, and the International Laboratory for Research on Animal Diseases (ILRAD) are tying them together with PC-based LANs. In either case, the centre's network can be augmented to include a gateway program that provides desk-to-desk e-mail for all professionals. These gateway systems should increase both the effectiveness and the efficiency of message communications.

PC software for simplicity and fast searching

For those who are able to use the system without an intermediary, the interaction with CGNET is a kind of typewritten conversation. The user types a command line to the system, then hits the return key; the system then responds by displaying one or more lines of information, one after the other, on the user's computer screen. The user and the system alternate, taking turns placing complete lines of text on the bottom of the user's screen.

This type of "conversational computing" originated in the late 1960s and has been a very durable feature of computer use for two decades. It remains the interaction style of choice for several kinds of information retrieval and programming. It is less than ideal, however, for many ordinary computer tasks. Many people are now familiar with word processing and spreadsheet calculation on PCs, where the style of interaction is very different. In those situations, the entire screen is filled with information and constantly kept up to date by the system. The user can move a cursor anywhere on the screen and change it with a few keystrokes, rather than composing a command. On PCs, users expect the system to respond and take action after any key is struck. This faster and highly visual style of interaction with computers is "natural" for word processors and spreadsheets and is radically different from the conversational computing that is common on most e-mail systems.

The natural style of user interaction for message transfer on computers is quite different from conversational computing. For most users, message transfer resembles word processing, with easy editing of messages and very simple, short commands to read and send messages. It usually also has some facilities for searching and retrieving old messages. One program with these features was introduced on CGNET in 1988. It included special features to help with the transfer of data files and documents, and it could be tailored to suit users of different word processors. Although it was not well suited for users who had difficult local telephone systems, it was a step in the right direction. This new sort of software should make e-mail considerably easier to use.

Most centres also need to maintain archives of their communications and documents. With an increasing proportion of those communications being carried electronically, it becomes appropriate to look for software that will store and index this material. Technological progress has greatly increased the storage capacity of small computers and allowed them to hold volumes of documents in a form that can be searched quickly. Software is already available to store and search e-mail messages; future software will allow scanned documents (such as paper or facsimile correspondence) to be included in these archives. An added bonus of using this type of software is that the productivity of busy professionals is increased when they can find relevant documents quickly.

Novel telecommunications services

A number of capabilities could be added to CGNET to tailor accounts even more closely to users' needs. Low-volume users might benefit from a service that notified them when they had mail. They could be given a telephone number to call, where a computer-synthesized voice could tell them the status of their mailbox. Or, alternatively, low-volume users could receive a telephone call, a facsimile, or a telex telling them that they should check their boxes. This would minimize the problem of making an expensive phone call, only to discover there is no mail. Users in locations with difficult communication could automatically have their messages sent by telex or facsimile if they had not checked their mailboxes recently. Finally, users on leave could have their mail automatically forwarded to other destinations (to be handled by colleagues). All of these services are currently in use in various corporate communications services. They may not all be appropriate to the CGNET community, but many are likely to be tried on CGNET in the next few years.

Mailboxes for voice messages could also be used to complement an existing e-mail service. Many corporations use "voice-mail" systems to store spoken messages in individual "voice mailboxes." Like e-mail, the mailboxes in a voice-mail system are actually files in a computer; therefore, the mailbox computer can easily duplicate messages if they are intended for more than one person. Voice mail is especially useful for very busy or very mobile professionals who need to receive and send messages with a minimum of delay while they are on the road. It is also useful when large time differences are involved or when confidential messages must be passed. Voice mail requires only a telephone, not a computer; therefore, it can be easier than e-mail for transferring very simple messages. The downside to voice mail is that it is limited to spoken messages and the amount of information that can be transferred is very limited.

Each research centre could potentially adopt such a system for its internal use. For a voice-mail system to effectively serve the CGNET community as a whole, a central facility would need to be located in a country that could be easily reached from all others. It might also be a good idea to have a few voice-mailbox computers in different countries and to have some high-speed transfer method to connect them. Currently, such a facility must be considered as a speculative, but interesting, possibility.

Another more promising service would be to attach a "database server" to CGNET. Use of conventional database systems on CGNET has been limited (see Chapter 2). The barriers to using them include the complexity of conventional database inquiry languages, the expense of composing inquiries from locations with high communication costs, and the necessity of having someone develop and maintain the database.

"Database servers" are less prone to some of these problems because they accept inquiries as ordinary e-mail or telex messages and return their results as e-mail messages. Electronic Document Interchange (EDI) standards have been developed that make this type of inquiry feasible. A database server could not handle complex data such as general bibliographies, but it could be effective for data that have a simpler structure. In addition to simplifying the inquiry systems, database servers also reduce the cost of searching by permitting off-line compilation of the query and batched processing of the database search. If the database is maintained or published in other forms (such as in the mainframe computer of a centre or on CD-ROM) the problem of having a person maintain the data can also be eliminated.

Problems can still arise when distributing data on database servers. When the users of the database speak a different language than the developers, or when the users do not really understand the contents of the database, there are likely to be problems. Without some special software at the user's end, there may also be problems with users formulating their queries incorrectly. These information servers may therefore work best for simple compilations of textual data (for example, address lists or typewritten briefs describing national or international research). More complex data may require other means of distribution, such as on-line databases or CD-ROM technology.

CD-ROM: an alternative technology for database dissemination

CD-ROM was developed from audio compact disk technology and allows enormous amounts of data to be stored on a small, durable disk. CD-ROMs are likely to take on great importance as a key communication medium for the IARC community because they allow effective dissemination of databases at very low cost. If properly applied, they will complement and improve on-line mail communications.

A CD-ROM holds about 600 megabytes of data, equivalent to over

1 500 conventional floppy disks or as much as 200 000 printed pages. The data on a CD-ROM are duplicated onto a laminated aluminum surface and are virtually impossible to damage. Because the data are physically encoded and optically accessed, they are free of the errors that plague magnetic-based media.

Like their on-line counterparts, CD-ROM databases are accompanied by search and retrieval software that allows a user to peruse a subset of the database that matches specific criteria. To use a CD-ROM, an ordinary PC and a CD-ROM drive are needed. These drives now cost between 400 and 800 USD, and their price is dropping.

CD-ROMs have great potential to widely disseminate research results or institutional information at low cost. Unlike on-line databases, CD-ROMs can be used at any location where there is a computer, even where telecommunications are poor or nonexistent. Training is less of a problem with CD-ROMs than with on-line databases because it costs nothing to experiment. Users can also be assured that no action they take can possibly corrupt the data.

Creating a CD-ROM is relatively inexpensive. It typically costs under 30 000 USD for a single-disk project. This cost includes the cost of developing a retrieval interface, of licencing retrieval software, and of duplicating several hundred CDs. Additional copies cost only about 2 USD each if they are made during the main production run. Costs can be even lower with careful planning to combine several CD-ROM projects.

Distribution of CD-ROMs is also simple. After an application has been produced, copies can be made in a matter of days. Quarterly or annual updates to the database can be made in a week. The media is durable and inexpensive to ship around the world. In contrast, a paper-based publication is expensive to ship and often takes 6 months to 1 year to produce.

Numerous CD-ROMs are commercially available, including the CGIAR's 17-disk Compact International Agricultural Research Library (CIARL), which contains data and documents produced by the CGIAR centres between 1962 and 1986. Other commercially available CD-ROMs vary from general information (dictionaries, thesauruses, and style manuals) to scientific data (climate information and bibliographies produced by CGIAR, CIMMYT, the Commonwealth Agricultural Bureaux (CAB), the Royal Tropical Institute (KIT), and the United States National Agricultural Library). Possibilities for additional CD-ROM projects within the IARC community include distributing bibliographic databases, compiling and disseminating agricultural germplasm data, and producing training materials and institutional information.

The value of such data dissemination is potentially significant, especially when the recipient is a scientist at a remote location or an institution that has limited financial resources. In these cases, there is no other feasible and economic way to deliver large volumes of information to the scientists who need it because on-line searching will remain impractical for such recipients well into the foreseeable future.

Although CD-ROM technology offers great potential, not every application works well in CD form. The CD-ROM media is most useful for data sets that do not become outdated quickly. With stable data sets, updates can be made less frequently than with unstable data sets. Existing CD-ROM databases are commonly updated yearly or quarterly, although some commercial applications are updated monthly or weekly.

CD-ROMs can complement and build on the services of e-mail networks like CGNET. Because CD-ROM data are in computerized ("machine-readable") form, they can be easily duplicated and sent using e-mail. For example, one scientist with access to a CD-ROM can find the information and forward it to others within a region or within a research network. Advice on how to use the CD-ROM can be solicited and delivered as e-mail messages, especially for first-time CD-ROM users. If a user does not have the time, or is unwilling to learn how to use a CD-ROM database, it can still be of use: librarians on the e-mail network can conduct a search on their copy of the CD-ROM and deliver to the user specific instructions on how to get the information out of the CD-ROM. (This information is itself machine readable; therefore, with a little software development, these instructions could be directly executed by the user's CD-ROM software.)

An e-mail connection can also enhance the value of the CD-ROM database. Some recent CD-ROM products allow new information to be received using an on-line connection and added as an update to a CD-ROM database. Although the CD-ROM itself is not changed, the additional information is saved in the user's computer and is searched whenever the CD-ROM data is searched. E-mail can also be used to coordinate the collection of information for publication on a CD-ROM, especially when the users are in widely dispersed locations.

In summary, CD-ROMs will fill an important role by providing access to databases that CGNET and other on-line services have not accessed. The combination of e-mail and CD-ROM technology offers special promise for researchers in remote locations and for national research institutions.

Chapter 6

THE FUTURE OF ELECTRONIC
COMMUNICATION IN CGIAR

Earlier chapters focused on the history of electronic communication in CGIAR and on how this new mode of communication began to influence the way the institutions in the CGIAR community conducted their business. This chapter concentrates on the future role of electronic communication in CGIAR and places emphasis on the likely influence that further advances in information technology will have on the way CGIAR institutions will operate in the future.

The preceding chapters have illustrated that, like many innovations, CGNET faced initial resistance from its target community. To gain acceptance as a reliable communication mode, CGNET had to prove its practicality and cost effectiveness.

Some of the barriers that stood in the way of proving CGNET's practicality were physical and technological (such as incompatible equipment, unclear telephone lines, and inappropriate modems); others were human and psychological (such as untrained personnel, fear of computers, conservatism, and resistance to change). It took many CGIAR institutions 4 or 5 years to overcome these barriers and to accept CGNET as a mode of communication that was comparable with more traditional means. However, the task is not finished. A few centres (such as ICARDA) are not able to participate for political or technical reasons. Some of the centres that participate have not yet been able to take full advantage of the opportunities offered by this powerful tool.

Proving the cost effectiveness of CGNET was less difficult. After it became practical to use the network, participating CGIAR institutions could see the savings that CGNET offered compared with telex and overseas telephone calls. Improvements in transmission speed further reduced the initial costs; better equipment increased the reliability of electronic communication.

Since its initiation as a pilot project in 1983, CGNET has now gained general acceptance within CGIAR as a reliable mode of communication. Having become a part of CGIAR culture, electronic communication is likely to have a major influence on the way CGIAR institutions conduct their business in the future. The precise form this influence will take depends on changes that are now taking place both in information and electronic communications technology and in CGIAR.

Changes in Information Technology

CGNET was a byproduct of the information revolution that has swept the globe. The future directions of this revolution are clear — faster, cheaper, and more powerful computers and better telecommunications systems that can transmit much higher volumes of information to many more locations. Today's supercomputers will become tomorrow's desktop computers. Telecommunications links will be extended to increasingly remote locations and communication lines made of new materials will enable high-speed networking. In addition, the current advances in technology will enable conversion of various types of communication (speech, video, and text) into machine-readable form. Therefore, it will be possible to transmit at high speeds not only voice, data, and text, but also graphics and video images. Another change that offers great potential is applications software. The opportunities presented by more powerful computers will allow increased development and dissemination of expert systems based on artificial intelligence. It will also be possible to develop information systems many times the size of today's systems and make them available at the remotest locations around the globe.

Tomorrow's agricultural researchers will face a radically different work environment — one in which computers and electronic communication influence every aspect of their work. In addition, ease of electronic communication will influence the way institutions are organized and managed.

The Future of CGIAR

CGIAR itself is undergoing a significant transformation. The changes taking place in CGIAR have both a quantitative and a qualitative dimension. Quantitatively, CGIAR is on the way to becoming a comprehensive, global agricultural research system. Its overall mandate was expanded recently to include research on forestry and fisheries. CGIAR has also committed itself to placing greater emphasis on sustainability and natural resource management. As a result of these changes, the number of autonomous international centres supported by CGIAR has increased from 13 to 18, and more centres are likely to be added.

The qualitative changes taking place in CGIAR are found in the organization of CGIAR and the foci of individual centres; the way the centres are linking their activities to those of their clients and other stakeholders; and the way the centres organize and manage their affairs. From a structural standpoint, CGIAR appears to be moving toward having two different types of centres: one group of global subject matter institutes and another group of regional institutes with agroecological mandates. The subject matter institutes will continue to carry out strategic research on commodities, food policy, germplasm conservation, and other questions of global significance. In contrast, the research of the so-called "ecoregional" entities will not be limited to individual commodities or issue areas. Instead, these institutes will conduct strategic and applied research on various problems of significance in different agroecological regions.

If the existing proposals for structural change are accepted, both types of institutes would continue to play a "bridging role" between the advanced research institutions around the globe (located mostly in developed countries) and the agricultural research institutions in developing countries. Basically, the subject matter institutes would form a bridge between the advanced research institutions carrying out basic and strategic research and the CGIAR entities carrying out ecoregional research. The ecoregional entities, on the other hand, would play a bridging role between their client developing country research institutions and the CGIAR subject matter institutes. If CGIAR moves in this direction, it will become a more "interconnected" system, both internally and externally. The effectiveness of such a system will depend greatly on the efficiency of communication among the component entities.

The way the centres organize and manage their internal affairs in the future is likely to complement external structural changes. Greater focus on holistic approaches to natural resource management, and a greater emphasis on bringing staff closer to problems at the farm level, will require further decentralization of the ecoregional entities to locations within their respective regions. Networking among agricultural researchers has gained momentum in recent years as a cost-effective way to carry out international research and strengthen national institutions in developing countries. The number of international agricultural research networks initiated or facilitated by the centres is likely to increase, and the need for telecommunication links within these networks can be expected to grow. These changes would require improvements in centre-based electronic communications systems. These centre-based systems would almost certainly be part of a CGIAR-wide communication system like CGNET.

Opportunities and Challenges

The future success of CGIAR will depend to a large extent on its ability to integrate its various components and activities. Fortunately, the changes taking place in information technology will enable it to form and maintain the types of electronic communication networks that are a prerequisite for effective integration. Centres are increasingly using LANs to link their personnel and provide them with common access to resource materials. Connections between centres have also improved as more and more centres and branch offices have been brought on-line. In addition to facilitating system integration, these changes are likely to change the way CGIAR institutions conduct their business.

First, they make it possible to establish a system-wide information, communication, and decision-support system that could be used interactively by all components of CGIAR (donors, centres, client national institutions, other collaborating institutions, and the CGIAR's central units). This system would enable the donors and the clients of CGIAR centres to obtain comprehensive and up-to-date information on the products of the centres. In addition, each institution would be able to develop comprehensive customized subsystems to meet its own needs. These systems would enable researchers to obtain the information they need for their work and to communicate with other researchers instantly. Similarly, managers would have up-to-date information to facilitate their decision-making.

Second, the centres would be able to establish flexible work teams. As a person's location becomes less important, it is easier to set up "cluster organizations" for specific projects that involve staff from different organizations. Today's project-based organizations are likely to evolve into multiorganization teams. The traditional definition of an organization will begin to change, and the borders between organizations will start to disappear in much the same way as borders have disappeared in today's international networks.

The important question is what effect increased integration will have on the products of the centres. Because the research of the centres is geared mainly toward generating new or improved agricultural technology, the impact of new information technologies and modes of organization will be measured by their impact on the innovation process. Can we expect that increased links between centre staff and increased access to common information will improve the innovation process in the CGIAR system?

Evidence from private manufacturing enterprises that have integrated the efforts of different departments, such as design, engineering, manufacturing, and marketing, is suggestive. A review of the product-development processes in these firms indicates that application of new information technologies (and the resulting integration) has accelerated the process of innovation and development. In an analysis of information technology and organizational interdependence, Rockart and Short (1989) concluded that Black and Decker now brings new products to market in half the time it took before 1985 and pointed out that the Xerox Corporation and the Ford Motor Company claimed similar improvements in key product lines.

New information and electronic communications technologies are likely to generate similar effects within the CGIAR system, increasing the "innovation potential" of the centres. Flexible work teams made up of selected individuals from around the world, the ability to communicate quickly with peers, and improved access to common sources of information will help create research environments at the centres that are even more conducive to innovation.

CGIAR must address three important challenges to benefit fully from the opportunities offered by the advances in information technology:

➤ To benefit from the integrating effects of new information and communications technology, all components of CGIAR should participate fully in CGNET. This applies in particular to the donors, and to the clients of the centres in developing countries, whose participation to date has been extremely uneven. The donors could play an important role in facilitating the participation of agricultural research institutions from developing countries in CGNET.

➤ The CGIAR institutions will probably need to devote more resources to management of information and communication technologies (paralleling the trend in developed country organizations). As the new information and communication tools penetrate further into organizations, they will present new management challenges for CGIAR institutions.

➤ CGIAR should not allow itself to fall behind the changes that are taking place in communications technology in developed countries. Keeping up with these technical changes will require frequent upgrading of hardware and software and the recruitment of scientific and administrative staff who can take full advantage of the new technologies.

At the same time, the communication technologies adopted by CGIAR institutions should not be inaccessible to their partners in developing countries. Because CGIAR institutions work in both developed and developing countries, the technologies they use should be chosen to enable easy communication among all parties. CGNET's recent emphasis on internetworking, which includes a gateway linking the Centres' campus networks with the Internet academic network and with developing country commercial networks, is a good step in this direction. The publication of CGIAR documents and databases on CD-ROM is another appropriate application of information technology to developing country settings.

In the final analysis, the impact of the new information and communication technologies that the CGIAR institutions adopt will be measured by their contribution to the effectiveness and efficiency of these institutions. If these technologies can shorten the research process, increase the probability of generating agricultural innovation, or lead to administrative efficiency, the investments will be well justified.

Its pioneering effort to establish the first international electronic communication network among public international organizations has demonstrated that CGIAR wishes to remain at the cutting edge of information technology, in much the same way as it has been (and continues to be) a leader in agricultural science. The momentum created in the 1980s to establish CGNET must now be applied to explore the opportunities soon to be offered by new technologies.

RESULTS OF 1983 SURVEY OF COMMUNICATION NEEDS OF CGIAR CENTRES

Administrative Applications

1. Travel and meetings database
2. Purchasing and order tracking
3. Supply sharing
4. Annual budgets and budget reviews
5. Periodic reviews (CGIAR Secretariat and TAC)
6. Board nominations
7. Improved liaison with remote offices
8. Donor liaison
9. Centre Directors' liaison
10. Liaison with Centre Board of Directors
11. General liaison, TAC
12. General liaison, CGIAR Secretariat
13. Recruitment
14. Contractor liaison
15. Fiscal reporting from remote sites

Information Services

1. Management of international VIP mailing lists (such as directors of national programs)
2. Remote printing and typesetting

3. News releases and announcements
4. Access to computer-based translation service
5. On-line newsletter(s)
6. Public relations and communications officers user group
7. Distribution of press clippings and on-line press digest
8. Internal CGIAR project description distribution
9. Coordination of "audience" directories
10. Joint authorship and conveyance of newsletter articles
11. Coordinated sales and order processing for publications

Library Services

1. Librarian/information officers user group
2. On-line intermediary services for assistance in performing bibliographic database searches
3. Interlibrary loan and cooperation services for CGIAR centre libraries and national programs
4. Coordinated cataloging and abstracting services among libraries
5. Establishment of on-line information analysis centres within CGIAR
6. On-line bibliographic search services
7. On-line document retrieval
8. On-line document ordering
9. Interlibrary coordination
10. CGIAR system publication awareness
11. Shared database coordination with other centres
12. Provision of selective dissemination

Specialized Databases

1. Germplasm database
2. Training materials and methods database
3. Trainee tracking database
4. Crop disease surveillance database
5. Quarantine database

6. Résumé database (candidates for staff)
7. Funding sources database
8. On-line directories of CGIAR personnel, national programs, board members, and donors
9. Database on application software relevant to CGIAR centres

Computer Services

1. Liaison with computer centre managers
2. Access to current awareness services and consultants
3. On-line transfer of software
4. Shared library of application software (mainframe and micro-computer)

Scientific Programs

1. Joint research with remote locations
2. Transfer of machine-readable data from remote sites
3. On-going "conferences" among special interest groups
4. International nurseries
5. Awareness of important conferences and meetings
6. Access to specialized analysis services
7. Exchange of informal scientific information among scientific staff
8. Joint authorship of scientific papers and reports

Table A1. CGIAR communication expenses and volume.

Category	Monthly average (per centre)	Monthly total (15 centres)	Annual total
Expenses (USD)			
International telephone	2 965	44 475	533 700
Telex	2 234	33 510	402 120
Telegraph	1 640	24 600	295 200
Letters	1 731	25 965	311 580
Documents	2 452	36 780	441 360
Subtotal	11 022	165 330	1 983 960
Travel	55 394	830 912	9 970 944
Total	66 416	996 242	11 954 904
Volume (no.)			
International telephone	120	1 800	21 600
Telex	342	5 130	61 560
Telegraph	177	2 560	30 720
Letters	2 025	30 375	364 500
Documents	2 679	40 185	482 220

Table A2. Scientific and administrative communication needs
ranked in order of importance.

Communication need	Rank	
	Scientific staff	Administrative staff
Access to remote information (databases)	1	6
International e-mail	2	2
Ability to send facsimiles of documents or letters to international locations	3	3
Ability to reduce international telephone costs	4	5
Statistical analysis	5	7
Word-processing	6	4
E-mail within country	6	9
Ability to manipulate centre financial information	7	1
Direct access to telex	8	9
Other	9	10
E-mail within the centre	10	8

Table A3. Scientific and technical information needs
ranked in order of importance.

Information need	Rank
Identify scientific and technical publications relevant to centre research	1
Obtain in complete form scientific and technical publications	2
Keep aware of recent developments	3
Find specific facts	4
Locate information for others	5
Find answers to specific questions	6
Identify new information sources related to centre research	7
Identify new material, methods, and procedures	8
Prepare reports, articles, and speeches	9
Keep aware of who is knowledgeable in particular areas	9
Evaluate new materials, methods, and procedures	10
Develop new problem-solving approaches	11
Maintain friendly relations	11
Resolve conflicts	11

CGNET USERS LISTED BY COUNTRY

Argentina
UNDP.FO.ARG

Australia
ACIAR
CSIRO
PLAN-ANO

Bahrain
UNDP.FO.BAH

Bangladesh
FORD-DHAKA
UNDP.FO.BGD

Barbados
UNDP.FO.BAR

Belgium
PLAN-BNO

Benin
IITA-BENIN

Bhutan
FAO-BHU
UNDP-FO.BHU

Bolivia
PROINPA-BOLIVIA

Botswana
UNDP.FO.BOT

Brazil
FORD-RIO
UNDP.FO.BRA

Bulgaria
UNDP.FO.BUL

Burkina Faso
IIMI-BURKINA
UNDP.FO.BKF

Burundi
UNDP.FO.BUR

Cambodia
IRRI-CMB
UNDP.FO.CAM

Cameroon
CIP-BAMENDA
IITA-HUMID
NCRE
UNDP.FO.CMR

Canada
IDRC
PLAN-CNO
VANCOUV-RES

Cape Verde
UNDP.FO.CVI

Central African Republic
UNDP.FO.CAR

Chile
FAO-CHI
FORD-CHILE
UNDP.FO.CHI
UNDP.FO.CHI1

China
FORD-BEIJING
IBPGR-CAAS
UNDP.FO.CPR
WINROCK-BEIJING

Colombia
CIAT
UNDP.FO.COL

Costa Rica
CIAT-CR
CIMMYT-CR
IBPGR-SHU-CR
UNDP.FO.COS

Côte d'Ivoire
FAO-IVC
IIRSDA
RTI-ABIDJAN
UNDP.FO.IVC
WARDA

Cuba
FAO-CUB

Cyprus
UNDP.FO.CYP

Dominican Republic
CIM-CESDA
FAO-DOM
PLAN-AZUA
PLAN-SANTO
UNDP.FO.DOM

Ecuador
CIP-QUITO
PLAN-QUITO

Egypt
ACDI-EGYPT
FAO-EGY
FORD-CAIRO
ICARDA-CAIRO
IDRC.MERORIRRI-CAIRO
PLAN-CAIRO
SUEZ-CANAL-U
UNDP.FO.EGY

El Salvador
CIM-SALVADOR
PLAN-CHALATENANGO
PLAN-LA-LIBERTAD
PLAN-SALVADOR
UNDP.FO.ELS

Equatorial Guinea
UNDP.FO.EQG

Estonia
UNDP.FO.EST

Ethiopia
ILCA
UNDP.FO.ETH

Fiji
UNDP.FO.FIJ

France
INIBAP

Gabon
UNDP.FO.GAB

Gambia
UNDP.FO.GAM

Germany
PLAN-GNO

Ghana
FAO-GHA
SIGMA1-GHA
UNDP.FO.GHA

Guatemala
CIAT-GUATEMALA
CIMMYT-GUATEMALA
PLAN-AMATITLAN
PLAN-PROGRESO
PLAN-ZACAPA
UNDP.FO.GUA

Guinea Bissau
UNDP.FO.GBS

Guyana
UNDP.FO.GUY

Haiti
PLAN-CDB
UNDP.FO.HAI1

Honduras
CIM-HONDURAS
PLAN-SANTAROSA
PLAN-SPS
PLAN-TEGUCIGALPARUN
DP.FO.HON

India
CIP-DELHI
FAO-IND
FORD-DELHI
IBPGR-DELHI
ICRISAT
IDRC.SARO
PLAN-BOMBAYI
PLAN-DELHI-CASP
PLAN-DELHI-DES
PLAN-DELHI-WAFD
UNDP.FO.IND
WINROCK-DELHI

Indonesia
CIFOR
CIP-BOGOR
CIP-INDONESIA
FAO-IPM
FG-INDONESIA
FORD-JAKARTA
PLAN-EASTJAVA
PLAN-KUPANG
PLAN-LOMBOK
PLAN-SS
PLAN-YOGYAKARTA
RTI-INDO
UNDP.FO.INS
WINROCK-JAKARTA
WINROCK-SALATIGA

Italy
IBPGR
IFAD
TAC

Jamaica
UNDP.FO.JAM

Japan
UNDP.FO.JPN

Kenya
CABI-IIBC-KENYA
CIP-NBO
FAO-KEN
FORD-NBO
ICIPE
ICRAFRICRAF-EMBU
ICRAF-MASENO
ICR-EARSAM
IDRC.EARO
ILCA-MOMBASA
ILCA-NAIROBI
ILRAD
PLAN-EMBU
PLAN-KIAMBU
PLAN-MERU
PLAN-TAITA
ROCKEFELLER-NBO
TSBF

UNDP.FO.KEN
UNDP.FO.OPSKEN
UNEP
USAID-KENYA

Korea (Republic of)
RDA
UNDP.FO.ROK

Kuwait
UNDP.FO.KUW

Malawi
CIAT-AFRICA

Malaysia
IIBC-MALAYSIA
MARDI
UNDP.FO.MAL
UPM

Maldives
UNDP.FO.MLD

Mali
IER-MALI
ILCA-BAMAKO

Mauritania
UNDP.FO.MAU

Mexico
CETEI
CIMMYT
FG-MEXICO
FORD-MEXICO
ROCKEFELLER-MX
UNDP.FO.MEX

Morocco
IAV
IAV.LIBRARY
IIMI-RABAT
UNDP.FO.MOR
USAID-RABAT

Mozambique
UNDP.FO.MOZ

Namibia
UNDP.FO.NAM

Nepal
CIMKAT
IIMI-NEPAL
UNDP.FO.NEP

Netherlands
ISNAR
PLAN-NLNO
WAU.LIBRARY

Nicaragua
UNDP.FO.NIC

Niger
ICRISATSC
IIMI-NIGER
UNDP.FO.NER

Nigeria
IITA
ILCA-KADUNA
UNDP.FO.NIR

Pakistan
FAO-PAK
IIMI-PAK
UNDP.FO.PAK

Panama
CIM-PANAMA
UNDP.FO.PAN

Papua New Guinea
UNDP.FO.PNG

Paraguay
CIM-PARAGUAY

Peru
CIAT-PUCALLPA
CIP
FAO-PER
FORD-LIMA
UNDP.FO.PER

Philippines
FAO-PHI

FORD-MANILA
ICLARM
IRRI
PLAN-BICOL
PLAN-BAGUIO
PLAN-CALAPAN
PLAN-CEBU
PLAN-PHILIPPINE
PLAN-SEARO
UNDP.FO.PHI
WINROCK-MANILA

Poland
UNDP.FO.POL

Rwanda
CIAT-RWANDA
CIP-RWANDA
UNDP.FO.RWA

Samoa
UNDP.FO.SAM

Saudi Arabia
UNDP.FO.SAU

Senegal
IDRC.WARO
IIEN.SENEGAL
UNDP.FO.SEN
WINROCK-SENEGAL

Singapore
IBPGR-SHU-SING
IDRC.ASRO

Somalia
FAO-SOM

Sri Lanka
IIMI
PLAN-BADULLA
PLAN-KANDY
UNDP.FO.SRL

Switzerland
DHAGVA
SFIT
UNDP.GENEVA

Taiwan
AVRDC

Tanzania
CIAT-AFRICA
PLAN-SALAAM
UNDP.FO.URT

Thailand
CIAT-BANKOK
CIMMYT-BANGKOK
FAO-RAPA
IBSRAM
IRRI-BANGKOK
PLAN-BANGKOK
PLAN-KK
PLAN-MAHA
PLAN-UDORN
ROCKEFELLER-TH
UNDP.FO.THAI

Togo
FG-TOGO
IFDC-TOGO
UNDP.FO.TOG

Trinidad and Tobago
CABI-IIBC-CLAS
UNDP.FO.TRI

Tunisia
CIP-TUNIS
UNDP.FO.TUN

Turkey
CIMMYT-TURKEY
FAO-TUR
ICARDA-TURKEY
UNDP.FO.TUR

Uganda
CIAT-UGANDA

ICRAF-KABALE
UNDP.FO.UGA

United Kingdom
CABI
GCRI
ECTOL
IBPGR-SHU-KEW
MSDN
NEW.SCIENTIST
NIAB
PLAN-UKNO
PRC
SCRI

United States
AGCOM
AID.IARC
AID.ST.AG
ACDI.ASPAC
ARD/W
BURNESS
CGIAR
CIAT-MIAMI
CITI
CORNELL
DIVERSITY
FAO-LUNO
FG-CONNECTICUT
FG-HQ
FORD
GRIN
HI-AGRON-SS
IBSNAT
IFAR
IFDC
IIE
IFPRI
INTSORMIL
NAL-LENDING

NIFTAL
OSU-IPPC
PLAN-USNO
PURDUE-RIISP
ROCKEFELLER
RODALE
RTI-CIDRRTI-ORC
SIGMA1
TAC-UCD
TROPSOILSRUNDP
WINROCK
WORLDBANK-INQUIRY

Uruguay
IDRC.LARO
IFDC.URUGUAY
UNDP.FO.URU

Venezuela
UNDP.FO.VEN

Vietnam
UNDP.FO.VIE

Yemen
UNDP.FO.YEM

Zimbabwe
CIMZIM
FAO-ZIM
ICRISATZW
ILCA-HARARE
PLAN-BULAWAY
PLAN-KWEKWE
PLAN-MASVINGO
PLAN-MUTARE
PLAN-TONGOGARA
UNDP.FO.ZIM

CGIAR AND OTHER MAJOR CGNET USERS

ACIAR	Australian Centre for International Agricultural Research
AVRDC	Asian Vegetable Research and Development Center
CABI	Commonwealth Agricultural Bureaux International
CGIAR	Consultative Group on International Agricultural Research
CIAT	International Center for Tropical Agriculture
CICP	Consortium for International Crop Protection
CIDA	Canadian International Development Agency
CIMMYT	International Centre for Maize and Wheat Improvement
CIP	International Potato Center
Citibank	Citibank International Services
Cornell	Cornell University
CSI	CGNET Services International
CSIRO	Commonwealth Scientific and Industrial Research Organization
FAO	Food and Agriculture Organization of the United Nations
Ford	Ford Foundation
Hawaii	University of Hawaii
IBPGR	International Board for Plant Genetic Resources

IBSNAT	International Benchmark Sites Network for Agrotechnology Transfer
IBSRAM	International Board for Soil Research and Management
ICIPE	International Centre of Insect Physiology and Ecology
ICLARM	International Center for Living Aquatic Resources Management
ICRAF	International Centre for Research in Agroforestry
ICRISAT	International Crops Research Institute for the Semi-Arid Tropics
IDRC	International Development Research Centre
IFDC	International Fertilizer Development Center
IFPRI	International Food Policy Research Institute
IIE	Institute for International Education
IIMI	International Irrigation Management Institute
IITA	International Institute of Tropical Agriculture
ILCA	International Livestock Centre for Africa
ILRAD	International Laboratory for Research on Animal Diseases
INTSORMIL	International Sorghum and Millet Research Institute, University of Nebraska
IPPC	Oregon State University
IRRI	International Rice Research Institute
ISNAR	International Service for National Agricultural Research
NCRE	National Cereals Research and Extension Project, Cameroon (IITA, Ibadan)
NIFTAL	Nitrogen Fixation by Tropical Agricultural Legumes Research Program, University of Hawaii
Nottingham	University of Nottingham
PLAN	Foster Parents Plan International
Purdue	Purdue University
Queensland	Plant Pathology Bureau

RDA	Rural Development Administration, Republic of Korea
Rockefeller	Rockefeller Foundation
Rodale	Rodale Institute
SFIT	Swiss Federal Institute of Technology
SIGMA-1	Sigma-1 Consulting
SOILCON	Soil Conservation Research Branch, Queensland
TAC	Technical Advisory Committee
UNDP	United Nations Development Programme
USAID	United States Agency for International Development, Science and Technology, Directorate for Food and Agriculture, IARC Relations
USDA	United States Department of Agriculture, Database Unit
WARDA	West Africa Rice Development Association
WAU.LIBRARY	Wageningen Agricultural University Library (Pudoc)
Winrock	Winrock International
World Bank	International Bank for Reconstruction and Development

Organizations that Can Be Reached Using CGNET

AFRUS	Agriculture and Food Research, Unit of Statistics, Edinburgh
AG-BIOTECH	United States Department of Agriculture, Office of Biotechnology
GCRI	Glasshouse Crops Research Institute, West Sussex, UK
IFAR	International Fund for Agricultural Research
NAL	United States National Agricultural Library
SCRI	Scottish Crop Research Institute
USAID.CDIE	United States Agency for International Development, Center for Development Information and Evaluation

Agricultural Research Institutes and Universities that Can Be Reached Using CGNET

Dalhousie University
Michigan State University
National Institute of Agricultural Botany, Cambridge, UK
New Scientist Magazine
North Carolina State University, Economics Department
Oklahoma State University
Plant Breeding Institute, Cambridge, UK
Poultry Research Centre, Edinburgh, UK
Rutgers University, International Agriculture and Food Program
University of Arkansas
University of California, Davis
University of Connecticut, Agricultural Experiment Station
University of Delaware, College of Agricultural Science
University of Georgia
University of Illinois, International Agricultural Programs
University of Maine, Office of Research and Development
University of Maryland, College of Agricultural and Life Sciences
University of Maryland, Institute of Applied Agriculture
University of Massachusetts, College of Food and Natural Resources
University of Mississippi, International Programs
University of Missouri, Atmospheric Sciences
University of Missouri, International Programs
University of New Hampshire
University of North Carolina, Agricultural Economics Department
University of North Carolina, Genetics Department
University of Rhode Island, College of Resource Development
University of Vermont, College of Agricultural and Life Sciences
University of West Virginia, College of Agriculture and Forestry

Appendix 4

COUNTRIES WITH DOMESTIC DATA NETWORKS OR REVERSE CHARGING OF ACCESS

CGNET Access Using National Data Networks

Antigua and Barbuda [c]	Finland [b]	*Korea (Republic of)
Argentina [c]	*France [b,c]	Kuwait
*Australia [b,d]	French Guiana	Liechtenstein
Austria	French Polynesia	Luxembourg
Bahamas	Gabon	*Malaysia
Bahrain [c]	Gambia	Martinique
Barbados [c]	*Germany [b,c]	Mauritius
*Belgium [b,c]	Greece [c]	*Mexico [b]
Bermuda [c]	Greenland	Montserrat
Brazil [b]	Guadeloupe	Namibia
*Cameroon	Guam	*Netherlands [b,c]
*Canada [a,b]	*Guatemala [c]	New Caledonia
Cayman Islands [c]	*Honduras [c]	*New Zealand
*Chile	Hong Kong [b,d]	*Niger
*China	Hungary	Norway [b]
*Colombia [c]	Iceland	Pakistan
*Costa Rica	*India	*Panama [c]
*Côte d'Ivoire	*Indonesia	*Papua New Guinea
Cuba	Iraq	*Peru [c]
Curaçao	Ireland	*Philippines [c]
Denmark [b]	Israel [c]	Portugal
Djibouti	*Italy [b]	Puerto Rico [b]
*Dominican Republic [c]	Jamaica [c]	Qatar
*Egypt [c]	Japan [b,c]	Réunion
*El Salvador	Jordan	Russia
Faroe Islands	*Kenya	Saint Kitts

Saint Lucia	Sweden [b]	*United Kingdom [a,c,d]
Saint Vincent	*Switzerland [b,c]	*United States [a]
Saipan	*Taiwan [c]	*Uruguay
San Marino	*Thailand [c]	Vanuatu
Saudi Arabia	*Togo	Virgin Islands, UK
*Senegal	Tortola	Virgin Islands, USA [c]
*Singapore	Trinidad and Tobago	Yugoslavia
South Africa [b]	*Turkey	*Zimbabwe
*Spain [b]	Turks and Caicos Islands	
*Sri Lanka	United Arab Emirates	

CGNET Access Using IDD

*Bangladesh	*Haiti	*Nepal
*Burkina Faso	*Malawi	*Nigeria
*Cambodia	*Mali	*Paraguay
*Ethiopia	*Morocco	*Tunisia

Note: Countries preceded by an asterisk (*) are CGNET users currently on-line.

[a] Domestic reverse-charged access available.

[b] INFONET reverse-charged access available.

[c] TYMUSA reverse-charged access available.

[d] CGNET premium reverse-charged access available.

Acronyms and Abbreviations

ACIAR	Australian Centre for International Agricultural Research
AIDAB	Australian International Development Assistance Bureau
AVRDC	Asian Vegetable Research and Development Center
CAB	Commonwealth Agricultural Bureaux
CAD	Canadian dollar
CBMS	computer-based messaging system
CD-ROM	compact disk — read-only memory
CGIAR	Consultative Group on International Agricultural Research
CGNET	Consultative Group on International Agricultural Research Electronic Mail Network
CIARL	Compact International Agricultural Research Library
CIAT	International Center for Tropical Agriculture
CIDA	Canadian International Development Agency
CIMMYT	International Centre for Maize and Wheat Improvement
CIP	International Potato Center
CIPAV	Centro para la Investigación Sistemas Sostenibles Agropecuarios
CSI	CGNET Services International
CTA	Technical Centre for Agricultural and Rural Cooperation
DNA	deoxyribonucleic acid

EARN	European Academic Research Network
EDI	Electronic Document Interchange
EIES	Electronic Information Exchange System
FAO	Food and Agriculture Organization of the United Nations
GTZ	German Agency for Technical Cooperation
IARC	international agricultural research centre
IBPGR	International Board for Plant Genetic Resources
IBSRAM	International Board for Soil Research and Management
ICARDA	International Center for Agricultural Research in the Dry Areas
ICLARM	International Center for Living Aquatic Resources Management
ICRAF	International Center for Research in Agroforestry
ICRISAT	International Crops Research Institute for the Semi-Arid Tropics
IDD	international direct dial
IDRC	International Development Research Centre
IFDC	International Fertilizer Development Center
IFPRI	International Food Policy Research Institute
IIMI	International Irrigation Management Institute
IITA	International Institute of Tropical Agriculture
ILCA	International Livestock Centre for Africa
ILRAD	International Laboratory for Research on Animal Diseases
IMF	International Monetary Fund
IRRI	International Rice Research Institute
ISNAR	International Service for National Agricultural Research
KIT	Royal Tropical Institute
LAN	local area network
MARDI	Malaysian Agricultural Research and Development Institute
MIT	Massachusetts Institute of Technology

OECD	Organisation for Economic Co-operation and Development
PAHO	Pan American Health Organization
PBX	Private Branch Exchange
PC	personal computer
PLAN	Foster Parents Plan International
PROINPA	Promotora Industrial Panamericana
PTT	post, telephone, and telegraph organization
RDA	Rural Development Administration (Republic of Korea)
REM	remote electronic meeting
RTI	Research Triangle Institute
TAC	Technical Advisory Committee
TNC	terminal node controller
UNCED	United Nations Conference on Environment and Development
UNDP	United Nations Development Programme
USAID	United States Agency for International Development
USD	United States dollar
USDA	United States Department of Agriculture
VSAT	very small aperture terminal
WARC	World Administrative Radio Conference
WARDA	West Africa Rice Development Association

BIBLIOGRAPHY

Balson, D.; Drysdale, R.; Stanley, B., ed. 1981. Computer-based conferencing systems for developing countries. Report of a workshop held in Ottawa, Canada, 26–30 October 1981. International Development Research Centre, Ottawa, ON, Canada. IDRC-190e.

Bowers, K.; LaQuey, T.; Reynolds, J.; Roubicek, K.; Yuan, A. 1990. Where to start — a bibliography of general internetworking information; RFC 1175, FYI 3, CNRI, University of Texas, ISI, BBN, SRI, Mitre. ARPANET Network Working Group Request for Comments, Menlo Park, CA, USA.

Cerf, V. 1990. The Internet Activities Board; RFC 1160. ARPANET Network Working Group Request for Comments, Menlo Park, CA, USA.

Chorafas, D.N. 1991. Handbook of data communications and computer networks. 2nd ed. TAB Professional and Reference Books, Blue Ridge Summit, PA, USA.

Clark, M.P. 1991. Networks and telecommunications design and operation. John Wiley and Sons, New York, NY, USA.

Comer, D.E. 1981. Internetworking with TCP/IP. Volume I: Principles, protocols, and architecture. 2nd ed. Prentice Hall, Englewood Cliffs, NJ, USA.

Comer, D.E.; Stevens, D.L. 1991. Internetworking with TCP/IP. Volume II: Design, implementation, and internals. Prentice Hall, Englewood Cliffs, NJ, USA.

Doerfer, D. 1992. Network trouble shooting guide: DECNET Phase IV, TCP/IP FDDI. Prentice Hall, New York, NY, USA.

Frey, D.; Adams, R. 1989. A directory of electronic mail addressing and networks. 2nd ed. O'Reilly and Associates, Petaluma, CA, USA.

Froelich, F.E.; Kent, A. 1992. Encyclopedia of telecommunications. Marcel Dekker Inc., New York, NY, USA.

Hedrick, C.L. 1987. Introduction to the Internet protocols. Rutgers, The State University of New Jersey, New Brunswick, NJ, USA.

_____1988. Introduction to administration and management: introduction to administration of an Internet-based local network. Rutgers, The State University of New Jersey, New Brunswick, NJ, USA.

Heldman, R.K. 1992. Global telecommunications. McGraw-Hill, New York, NY, USA.

Hiltz, S.R.; Turoff, M. 1978. The network nation: human communication via computer. Addison-Wesley, Reading, MA, USA.

Horton, M.R.; Adams, R. 1987. Standard for interchange of USENET messages; RFC 1036. ARPANET Working Group Request for Comments, Menlo Park, CA, USA.

Jacobsen, O.; Lynch, D. 1991. A glossary of network terms; RFC1028, Interop Inc. ARPANET Working Group Request for Comments, Menlo Park, CA, USA.

Kille, S.E. 1986. Mapping between X.400 and RFC-822; RFC987. ARPANET Working Group Requests for Comments, Menlo Park, CA, USA.

_____1991. Addendum to RFC 987 (mapping between X.400 and RFC-822); RCF1208. ARPANET Network Working Group Request for Comments, Menlo Park, CA, USA.

Krol, E. 1989. The hitchikers guide to the Internet, RFC 1118, University of Illinois, Urbana. ARPANET Network Working Group Request for Comments, Menlo Park, CA, USA.

Lane, E.; Summerhill, C. 1992. An Internet primer for information professionals: a basic guide to Internet networking technology. Meckler Corporation, Westport, CT, USA.

LaQuey, T.L. 1990. The user's directory of computer networks. Digital Press, Burlington, MA, USA.

Lindsey, G. 1987. The Green Revolution. Kermit News, 2(1), 4–5.

Malkin, G.; Marine, A. 1991. Answers to commonly asked "new Internet user" questions; RFC1206 FYI 4, FTP Software Inc., SRI, ISI. ARPANET Network Working Group Request for Comments, Menlo Park, CA, USA.

Malkin, G.; Marine, A.; Reynolds, J. 1991. Answers to commonly asked "experienced Internet user" questions; RFC1207 FYI 7, FTP Software Inc., SRI, ISI. ARPANET Network Working Group Request for Comments, Menlo Park, CA, USA.

McNamara, J.E. 1985. Local area networks: an introduction to the technology. Digital Press, Burlington, MA, USA.

Mitchell, W.; Hendricks, R.; Sterry, L. 1992. Telecommunications: systems and applications for business. Paradigm Publishing International, Eden Prairie, MN, USA.

Pooch, U.W. 1992. Telecommunications and networking. CRC Press, Boca Raton, FL, USA.

Quarterman, J.S. 1990. The Matrix: computer networks and conferencing systems worldwide. Digital Press, Burlington, MA, USA.

Quarterman, J.S.; Hoskins, J.C. 1986. Notable computer networking. Communications of the ACM, 29(10), 932–971.

Rapaport, M. 1991. Computer mediated communications: bulletin boards, computer conferencing, electronic mail, and information retrieval. John Wiley and Sons, New York, NY, USA.

Rockart, J.; Short, J. 1989. IT in the 1990s: managing organizational inter-dependence. Sloan Management Review, 30(2), 7–17.

Rose, M.T. 1991. The simple book: an introduction to management of TCP/IP-based Internets. Prentice Hall, Englewood Cliffs, NJ, USA.

_____ 1992. The little black book: mail bonding with OSI services. Prentice Hall, Englewood Cliffs, NJ, USA.

Socolofsky, T.; Kale C. 1991. A TCP/IP tutorial; RFC1180. ARPANET Network Working Group Request for Comments, Menlo Park, CA, USA.

Tanenbaum, A.S. 1989. Computer networks. 2nd ed. Prentice Hall, Englewood Cliffs, NJ, USA.

Williams, B. 1992. A directory of computer conferencing in libraries. Meckler Corporation, Westport, CT, USA.

About the Institution

The International Development Research Centre (IDRC) is a public corporation created by the Parliament of Canada in 1970 to support technical and policy research to help meet the needs of developing countries. The Centre is active in the fields of environment and natural resources, social sciences, health sciences, and information sciences and systems. Regional offices are located in Africa, Asia, Latin America, and the Middle East.

About the Publisher

IDRC Books publishes research results and scholarly studies on global and regional issues related to sustainable and equitable development. As a specialist in development literature, IDRC Books contributes to the body of knowledge on these issues to further the cause of global understanding and equity. IDRC publications are sold through its head office in Ottawa, Canada, as well as by IDRC's agents and distributors around the world.